How to **Succ**

Separation & Divorce

FAY PETCHER

A relationship and divorce coach as
well as someone who's done it twice!!

Published by Goldcrest Books International Ltd
www.goldcrestbooks.com
publish@goldcrestbooks.com

ISBN: 978-1-913719-18-0
eISBN: 978-1-913719-19-7

*Dedicated to my children, Lucy and Toby,
who make me proud each and every day.*

CONTENTS

PREFACE

I am writing this book three years after my second marriage breakdown. Over the years, I had experienced infidelity, emotional abuse, narcissism, trauma (both physical and mental) as well as other mental health issues. I had two children, with two different dads.

I was like an injured bird, coming out of a gilded cage. I didn't know how to behave like a bird let alone how or where to fly. I didn't like myself and carried a huge, black ball of shame, guilt, fear and judgement – from myself and others – around with me. My self-esteem had vanished. I was existing on a very primal level. To say that I had hit rock bottom was an understatement.

I was suffering with anxiety, panic attacks and hypervigilance, which caused havoc with both my physical and emotional well-being. I couldn't rest, sleep or eat. If I was triggered (and that happened on a daily basis) I would go into 'flight or fight' mode and the whole vicious cycle would start again.

Three years on, writing this book during the COVID-19 outbreak, lots of people are suffering within their relationships, whether from abuse, lack of connection or conflict, and many will decide to divorce when we all get back to normal.

But I can honestly say that I am the happiest I have ever been. My children are happy and settled and I have a working relationship with both their fathers.

I can now look in the mirror and say that I love the person looking back at me. I know who I am and what I want from the rest of my life.

I have pushed myself out of my comfort zone, experienced new things, travelled, met new and interesting people and learned about myself on a much deeper level. As well as being a teacher, I became a divorce and relationship coach.

I am now in a happy, respectful and supportive relationship where I am not expected to justify who I am, how I want to be or what I want to do. I finally feel free to be me.

Writing this book now feels right. I find myself at a point in my life where the book inside of me wants to be written. I want to give people who find themselves single again, hope for the future and the strength and inspiration to move forwards. I am living proof that it can be done!

Throughout the book, I will share with you some of my first-hand experiences, both triumphs and failures, as well as practical tips that work, anecdotes and quotes that have seen me through and some laugh-out loud moments.

If you are reading this book, I am excited for you. Even though you feel as if your world has come crashing down, you have no idea how much learning, growing, happiness and fulfilment is yet to come. I am not saying that this book is an easy read; it is not. Recovering from a break-up, separation or divorce is hard. You will have to look at yourself and think about your part in the break-up. You have to look deep inside to accept who you truly are and you may not like what you find. It's going to be tough, but who says getting what you want out of life is easy? All you have to do is just keep putting one foot in front of the other and keep moving forwards.

"It doesn't matter how slowly you go
as long as you don't stop."

Confucius

CHAPTER 1

Single

*You're single not because you are not good enough for
one, it's that you're too good for the wrong one.*

Chris Burkmenn

Let's not beat about the bush. Being single, when you thought
that you had your life mapped out with one person, is awful.
I'd even go as far as to say it's pretty shit. You will feel
enormous emotional and physical pain, which is why people
call it heartbreak. You will feel as if you are not whole any
more, as the person that has been by your side has now gone.
It's an odd feeling and you may feel as if you are living in a
parallel universe. I know I did.

Even if it was your decision to split, it doesn't make it any
easier. You will feel as if you are carrying around a large and
shameful sign that says: "I have failed!"

♥ You feel you have failed because you could not hold a
   relationship together.

♥ You feel you have failed because you were not good enough.

♥ You feel you have failed because you are not a couple any more.

♥ You feel you have failed because your children no longer have a proper family unit.

♥ You feel you have failed because you fell out of love with the person you thought you would love forever.

♥ You feel you have failed because you fell in love with someone else.

If your relationship ended suddenly, because your partner walked out, had an affair or even dumped you via text or email (yes it does happen), it will feel as if your whole life has imploded. You may trick yourself into thinking that it is all a joke and you are waiting for someone to say "Gotcha!"

Everything you thought to be true and safe is now gone. You go to bed at night and struggle to sleep. When you eventually do, and wake up again, the reality of your situation slaps you in the face. It's like Groundhog Day. In the early days of both my marriage break-ups, I used to love going to bed and eventually falling asleep. It would give me time to forget, time to dream nice dreams (although often they weren't), and when I woke up again the awful realisation would hit me that I was now on my own and I felt pretty depressed. I felt constantly sick and sleeping was my escape from it all.

The pain you will feel cannot be described unless you have been there; it is an actual physical pain at your very core, which can manifest itself into raw physical and/or emotional pain.

You may feel depressed, anxious or overwhelmed. You will most likely get physical symptoms like sickness, colds or even panic attacks.

Everyone reacts differently, no two break-ups are the same, so whatever you are feeling it's ok to feel that way, go with it, own it and then conquer it!

Yes, it's OK for me to say that, as I'm out the other end and I make it sound so simple. But the truth is that it's not; it's hard, it takes time and you will have moments when you feel that it has defeated you. But, trust me, you will get there.

The one thing I have ingrained in me, after my experiences, is that nothing lasts forever. Some things are fleeting and the only thing you can be certain of is that you were born, and you will eventually die. I can see that you're glad you bought my book! But what happens to you in between is uncertain. We do not have instructions to guide us through our life from birth until death. Nothing can be planned or taken for granted. Things happen in life to trip us up, hit us between the eyes, make us learn lessons (the good, the bad and the ugly) to shape us into the people we were meant to be or want to be.

Do I believe in fate and destiny? I'm not going to bore you with my spiritualism or belief system. What I do believe is that things happen for a reason and unless you learn the lessons you need to, things will repeat themselves until you do.

One of the biggest issues that comes with a break-up, separation or divorce is the fear of judgement. Judgement by yourself and others can bring up feelings like shame, inadequacy and low self-esteem – and that's before you start on the other emotions that are going to be making an appearance over the weeks and months to come. It's a little bit like coming off drugs or alcohol. You have to wean yourself off that person or go cold turkey. If you, or they, walked out of the door never to return, then you have to get used to not being in that person's life any more.

The stages that you will go through during a break-up are no walk in the park. You may get stuck at a stage, unable to move forwards. You may slip back into the previous stage, or you may be in more than one stage at the same time. Sounds great, doesn't it? Even a lobotomy sounds easier. But trust me, you will get through them and finally reach acceptance. Let things take their course. Don't try and rush because no one wins when things aren't done properly. I talk more about time in Chapter 7, but don't believe it when people say, 'Give it time' or 'In time things will get better'. Yes they do, but if you don't use the time wisely you may still be in the same place, physically and emotionally.

I had a client who was still lamenting about his life, his situation and questioning why things were not going in the direction that he wanted. I asked him why he thought this was (I knew what the problem was but wanted him to realise this). He shrugged his shoulders and said that he didn't have time to implement all the things we had put into his action plan as he had been working. It was easy for me but hard for him to realise that his life would not get better if he didn't put the effort into making changes. His life wasn't going to miraculously become fulfilled if he didn't work hard to turn it around. No one can change your life for you; you have to take steps to do it yourself and yes, it's hard, but the gains far outweigh the losses.

The main stages you will go through are:

Every self-help book and manual you read about how to get over heartbreak will have varying degrees of the same thing. One size does not fit all in this instance and you may feel things that are not on the list like jealousy, spite and hopelessness. That's OK. If it helps, jot down the other emotions that you feel. This is your break-up and they are your feelings. You will need to face them head-on and accept that this is how you feel, even if you don't like the feelings. No one can do this for you.

Be prepared for your mental health to take a serious knock. I'll talk more about this in a later chapter, but you may begin to suffer from depression, anxiety, panic attacks, CPTSD (complex post-traumatic stress disorder) or even self-harm or suicidal thoughts. If this does happen, seek support through mental health charities such as MIND, or your GP. You can get some free counselling, CBT (cognitive behaviour therapy) or other wellbeing therapies like EFT (emotional freedom technique – tapping) and Havening, where we stroke certain areas of our body while recalling traumatic events in order to heal ourselves and give ourselves self-love.

If you really need them, you can ask for sleeping pills or anti-depressants on a short-term basis just so that you can function.

One of my friends was prescribed sleeping pills for a short while. She was suffering from sleep deprivation due to worry over her finances. She had no clue how she was going to buy and maintain a home for her and her son. I'm not going to push my judgement and personal opinion on you and say, 'Do not take any medication'. Everyone is different and will struggle with different things. If you need help to get through each day, especially at the beginning, then ask for it.

I always tell people that getting over a break-up, separation or divorce is like climbing a mountain. I get them to visualise their mountain, give it a name if they want (but not their ex's!). We all have our own personal recovery mountain.

It is very large and steep. It has rocks all over it that are loose and may come off at any time and crash to the bottom. There is no clear path to the top. It is foggy and, in places, treacherous. You need to get to the top but you don't know how to and you don't know if you have the willingness or strength to conquer it. You may feel tempted to turn back, or find reasons not to start the climb because you know that it will take a long time. You may stumble, or go backwards, but you must keep pushing to move forwards even if it hurts like hell and you feel like giving up. You must carry on.

When you finally get to the top of your recovery mountain, you can rest, take a deep breath and look at the view. You can be proud of your achievement and you can stay at the top as long as you want.

The quote at the end of my preface: "It does not matter how slowly you go as long as you don't stop", was the quote that helped me get through each day. I had it on my phone and looked at it when I felt that I hadn't got anywhere or achieved anything. It kept me going.

Even if the steps you take are small, they are still forward steps. Small steps can, and will, lead to giant leaps.

The person you saw as 'your person' has now gone. It's like losing a piece of yourself and it feels lonely. Being alone when you have been part of a couple is hard. You feel as if you don't fit in anywhere.

Lying in bed, cooking and doing things on your own feels weird. The person you talked to when you had a bad day, went shopping at the supermarket with, is no longer there. Going alone to a party or family meal are all things that will seem strange. It may take you a while to be comfortable doing family things as a single person.

I remember the first Christmas after my first marriage breakdown. My daughter was two and I had moved to a new house and invited my parents round for Christmas dinner. Looking back at the photographs, I had staged it all to be a perfect Christmas: a tree, decorated table, the whole works! Looking back at the photographs that I put in an album entitled 'My New Life', I looked ill and so did my parents. My daughter was going to her dad's on Boxing Day and I wasn't sure how I felt about it. The next day, I dressed her up in her best dress, tied her hair in pigtails, smiled and waved when her dad came to pick her up. I felt like I was breaking inside, not because of my ex but because this was now going to be my Christmas, having to share my daughter with her dad. Not seeing my now-ex family, who I was very close to, upset me the most.

When it came to my second marriage breakdown, sharing my son with his dad was easier as I had already gone through it with my daughter. Juggling children, let alone at Christmas with two exes, can be difficult, but it seems to work. When they go to their dads' (and I'm lucky that they don't live too far away) I have already got plans, whether that is meeting up with friends, going out for a nice meal with my partner or going away for a few days.

Even though your life changes after separation and divorce, you will adapt to your circumstances and accept the changes that are now in front of you. You need to see change as an opportunity. It's an opportunity to live in a different and better way. Of course, you may not see it this way for quite a while. Healing after a break-up, separation or divorce can take anything from a few months to years. Some people never fully heal. I have met people who, years after their divorce, are still bitter about what happened, still in the same situation and still not wanting to change. If you're reading this book, you want to heal. This willingness to change and come out the other end a better and happier person will help you enormously. I am in awe of you already because you are ready to climb your own mountain.

Don't stop when it hurts, stop when it's done!

An unnamed woman Sherpa climbing K2

Top Tip

Give yourself time to acknowledge and work through all of the emotions that you may feel.

CHAPTER 2

Why?

Nothing hurts more than a heart left wondering why?

Anonymous

This is the big question that hangs over people's heads like a huge cloud after a break-up. It can consume your waking thoughts and your sleepless nights.

♥ Why has this happened to me?

♥ Why did things go wrong?

♥ Why couldn't I keep my relationship going?

♥ Why did I risk my relationship?

♥ Why did I end my relationship?

♥ Why didn't I do things differently?

♥ Why did my partner leave me?

💗 Why did I cheat?

💗 Why am I feeling this way?

💗 Why am I struggling with 'Why'?

And the list goes on ...

Relationships fail for many different reasons. There is no textbook reason as to why people split up, but I have tried to highlight some common reasons below. No two break-ups are the same, which again highlights the fact that all recoveries are, and will be, different.

You have grown apart

This usually happens when you have been together for a long time, met when you were young and probably raised a family together. Unfortunately, this wasn't me. I didn't get past 10 years with either of my marriages. Over time in longer relationships, you can become different people from when you first met. You realise that you want different things. Maybe your children have flown the nest and you are left wondering what the hell to do with the rest of your life – and it doesn't include your partner? You love them, like you love a comfy pair of slippers, but you're not in love with them and you don't want to spend the rest of your life with someone who you have seen every day for the past decade or two.

I coached a lady who was in this position. Her children were now adults and her youngest had just left to start a university degree. She had spent most of her marriage being a housewife, looking after the children, the house and making sure that everything was running smoothly. She had had the odd, part-time job, but her husband was the main bread winner and worked long hours.

She looked me straight in the eye and told me that she did not really love her husband anymore and she could not bear to spend the rest of her life with him. When I suggested that she sat him down and had an honest and frank conversation with him, she looked terrified and replied: "I can't do that! He might agree with me and then our marriage will be over."

I was a little perplexed with her response and asked her why that terrified her so much as surely it was what she wanted?

She went on to tell me that because of their financial position, she was worried about how she would survive if she didn't have the security that she was used to, and she had never really been out with anyone else, so was scared of what the future held.

I told her that the first conversation is always the hardest and that it was a good idea to seek legal advice before having the conversation with her husband, so that she knew what she would be entitled to after 30 years of marriage.

She wanted me to give her the answer, but I told her that I was not here to give her the answer, she had to find that herself. Taking the first step to a big life change is scary, but sometimes the scariest things bring the best reward. I told her to give herself time to process what we had spoken about, get advice from a solicitor and be kind to herself. I knew that if she took the first step, it would be the start of a very long road that would not always be smooth.

You want different things

Many couples can find that their lives and wants are no longer on the same page. This can happen if your career takes you away from home or you realise that you want to achieve something that your partner does not want to be a part of, such as taking a sabbatical from work to go travelling or wanting to move to a different country.

Big changes like these can highlight the problems in your relationship and make you realise that you are not as strong as you thought you were – made even more difficult if you have children.

One of the biggest differences can be children. I knew someone who had been married for ten-or-so years. They had been very happy, had good careers, a nice house, nice cars and quite a few holidays each year to very warm places. Jealous? I am!

Their marriage broke down because the woman decided that after originally saying that she didn't want children, she now did and in a big way. Her biological clock had sprung to life and was not going anywhere anytime soon. Her husband was dead set against the idea as he had been very clear about this from the moment they met. She hoped that he would change his mind and even thought about getting pregnant 'accidentally on purpose', which happens more than we realise. She was smart enough to realise that if she did this, he would be an absent father. She decided to cut her losses and move on. I think she is now happily married again with two children, running barefoot in the meadows ...

If this is you, keep going back to why you split up. Keep telling yourself it would never have worked in the long term, even if you really wanted it to, and now you are free to meet someone who wants and gets your aspirations and dreams of going trekking in Nepal or shark diving off the coast of Africa. It's OK to still love someone that you are no longer with, but you will find that someone or something will take the place of that love.

Tragedy

A family tragedy, such as a life-changing accident or a death, can break the strongest of couples. People find that the tragedy engulfs them, and they realise that they cannot be together because it is too painful, or because one person does not appreciate what the other is going through and cannot support them.

The death of a child (whether that is a child that has not yet been born or a child who has died due to an illness or accident) is the most painful thing you can go through as a parent. I have never experienced this and can only imagine what it feels like. I cried the other day at the courage a mum showed when supporting her son through terminal cancer.

Keeping a marriage together when faced with this must be extremely difficult if not impossible. You will either cling together for comfort or the grief will tear you apart as one or both of you try to make sense of what has happened and turn to other things as a way of coping.

When I was a student I worked in a shop. The couple that ran the shop were not married and over the months I worked there, they told me that they would never marry as one of them was already married. The woman's husband had been involved in a life-changing accident and was in a high dependency unit, paralysed from the chest down. She made no secret of the fact that she still loved her husband and felt a huge responsibility towards him. She would visit him every week but could not bear to divorce him. She had made a new life with her new partner, who was accepting of the situation.

Another example of this is something that I read in a newspaper article. It was about a person that was living two different lives. His first one was with his wife, again disabled due to a tragic accident, and his second one was with his lover. He spent most of his time with his wife as her carer, and some of the week at his lover's (telling his wife that he was working nights). He had no desire to leave his wife in the lurch, even though he wanted to be free to be with his lover. But he did not want to just abandon his wife as he loved them both in different ways.

Situations like these tell us that relationships are not cut and dried. They teach us that love is not demanding of others and if you love someone you will accept their personal situation whatever that may be.

If this is you, you will be feeling unsurmountable grief over your situation and your marriage breakdown. You owe it to yourself to keep going and you will eventually realise that you deserve to be happy.

Infidelity

I have lots of experience of this as both my marriages ended, in some part, due to the infidelity of both my husbands. I'm a big girl, no sympathy is needed as I dealt with it a long time ago.

Finding out that your partner has had an affair is awful. The loss of trust that comes with infidelity cannot be underestimated, especially if that person leaves you for their lover (now that is brutal, and yep, it happened to me).

When you find out about an affair, whether your spouse tells you or you find out another way (most people who conduct affairs have no desire to tell their other half), it is like being kicked in the gut again and again and again.

The ripples are felt not just by the betrayed person, but by the immediate and close family. The judgement placed on the person who had the affair is huge and the person who suffered will find that they have sympathy by the bucketload. I am not saying that this is right, it's just how it can be.

It's really hard for the betrayed person not to obsess over the 'other' person and try to find out who they are, where they work, what they look like and where they live. It can be all-consuming as the betrayed wonders what they didn't have that the other person did. If this is you, you may want to hunt them down and show them the damage that has been caused (especially if it has ripped your family apart) by getting revenge. Getting revenge is not always a good idea. I always say, you can't change what has happened, you can't make decisions for your ex. Feeling that you want revenge comes from the anger that you have inside. Cutting up your cheating partner's clothes, placing them in bin bags on the front lawn or painting, 'The driver of this car is a lying, cheating rat' may feel great at the time, but what purpose is it serving?

The saying: *Revenge is a dish best served cold* springs to mind here and what better revenge is there to have a happier and more fulfilled life afterwards?

One question I am asked a lot is, "Can couples heal after an affair?"

Yes, they can, but it is hard and takes a great amount of effort from both sides. You both need to know 100% that you want to make your relationship or marriage work. After an affair, emotions are running high. How on earth are you supposed to know the answer to that? A cooling-off period is definitely needed and being apart after an affair is a risk. The person who had the affair needs to fully understand the hurt that they have caused. The other person needs to accept why their partner had an affair in the first place and take some responsibility.

Both parties need to be honest and open in order to make it work. It also depends on the circumstances around what happened. Was it a drunken one-night stand or an affair that spanned years where there has been deceit and lies?

Most people who have children try and work through it, but once the trust has gone it is extremely difficult to rebuild and you will both become different people to who you were before.

Workplace affairs happen regularly as more and more people work longer hours and spend more time at work than they do at home. People are drawn together through having stressful jobs or working away, and the inevitable happens. In some companies, workplace affairs happen regularly. But the fallout that happens when the affair is disclosed is always bigger than the affair itself.

Some affairs do work out. One of my friends met her second husband through work. Even though she had not been married long, there was an instant connection. They tried hard to ignore the feelings that were growing between them, but they could not fight them. She divorced her husband and married her soulmate. They have gone on to have two children and a successful company. They have been married for many years and are still as happy now as when they first met.

When I found out about my second husband's affair, it was clear that he had not planned on being found out. We were on a family holiday with the children, and after finding out I spent most of the week trying to get a flight home. It was not a great situation to be in. We had to put on happy faces in front of the children, who were loving their holiday, when inside I was in shock and felt like my whole world had come crashing down around me for the second time.

My two exes are now married to the women that they had affairs with and I'm ok with that. It's their lives and I have to live mine. Am I married, I hear you ask? No, I'm still in the 'I want to be independent and free' stage. I do not want to conform to having a husband. I'm happy with a partner who has his own house and is as independent as me. But ask me again in 5- to 10-years' time and I might give you a different answer.

Abuse

Abuse, whether physical, coercive, emotional, psychological, economical, narcissistic or domestic, is wrong on every level.

And let's not be biased, it happens to both men and women – although statistics show that women are more likely to suffer abuse from their partners. The percentage of men who suffer abuse is rising. They are more likely to be abused by another male in their family dynamic rather than their partner (although it does happen).

The problem with abuse is that many victims do not realise that they are being abused if they are not being hit or beaten up. Victims of non-physical abuse will generally normalise the behaviour shown by their abuser and see it as the normal ups and downs of any relationship. Victims will make excuses for the abuser and overlook it as they are treated nicely in-between the abusive episodes.

Victims can also form co-dependency and unhealthy attachments to their abusers (a bit like Stockholm syndrome).

They see the abuse as a form of love from the abuser and why would they leave someone who loves them this much?

People who suffer abuse at the hands of their partner can suffer from low self-esteem, and feelings of worthlessness. They stay because they don't feel that they are good or worthy enough to move on and have another relationship. Or they are stuck because they haven't got the money to move out, which can be due to the abuser controlling the finances.

People who suffer abuse can develop mental health issues such as CPTSD, hypervigilance, anxiety, depression, self-harm and even suicidal thoughts.

Victims will very rarely leave their partners unless they have been forced to do so, either because they have ended up in hospital, are in fear of their lives or other people have stepped in to save them. Sometimes victims have no choice but to leave. They may have been dropped by their abuser to make room for someone new. This happens a lot in narcissistic abuse.

At the time of writing this (during the COVID-19 lockdown), a young nurse has been killed by her estranged partner in broad daylight. Cases of abuse are rising during lockdown and many victims are prisoners in their own homes. I have a couple of clients who are in abusive relationships but are not ready to leave their partners because they have children, or they are not sure what to do when they leave, or if they want to. All they know is that the way they are treated is wrong and it is slowly diminishing their self-worth and confidence. It is so important to realise that some victims do not think about leaving their partners until something major happens and they have no choice.

I left my second marital home because I didn't feel as if I had a choice. Being honest, at that time I would have stayed because I had no self-worth and so staying felt like the safe option. When I think back, it makes me feel ashamed. I can't bear thinking that I would still be in the marriage now, if I had not found out about his affair, or been given no option but to leave because he had someone new.

If you have left an abusive relationship or marriage, my heart goes out to you. With the right support, you will slowly and surely heal. Yes, your mountain is going to be higher and take longer to climb, but you will do it. I am in awe of your strength even though I don't know you. You are a warrior.

Sexuality

Many people leave their marriages or partners because they find out that their sexual orientation has changed, or they have been living a lie that they can no longer live with, or they want to explore their sexuality without lying to their partner.

We live in an age where it is becoming more acceptable to choose how you identify. Being gay, lesbian, bisexual, asexual, transsexual or transgender is no longer a subject to be brushed under the carpet.

This can be very hard for the people that are left behind (sometimes after many years of being together) but I always say, "It's better to live your truth than a lie."

Some couples stay together and become firm friends rather than sexual partners as finances and life makes splitting up very difficult. This sounds a good idea (especially when you have children) but starts to fall apart when one person wants to move forwards with someone else.

As I'm writing this, TV presenter Phillip Schofield has not long announced that he is gay and can't live a lie any longer. I feel desperately sorry for his situation and his family, but he won't be the first person to do this or the last.

I used to work with someone whose daughter ended her marriage for another woman.

Even though the family was deeply upset for their son-in-law, as they loved him as part of the family, they all pulled together to help them in any way that they could for the sake of their grandchildren who they loved dearly. Their daughter went on to marry her partner and their ex son-in-law found love in a new relationship. Even though it is hard, happiness and harmony can be achieved.

One little story that has sprung to mind as I am writing this is about when I was on a 'babymoon' in the Maldives – a holiday before my first child was born. Our maid told us that the hotel had had to move a groom from the island because his new wife had come back to their villa to find him in bed with another man. The uproar that ensued was so great that they had to split them up. It just shows that it can happen even when you think you have your life mapped out.

Midlife crisis

Hitting midlife can cause all manner of problems in a marriage or partnership.

You turn 50 and think, "Have I achieved what I set out to?" "Am I truly happy?" "Am I where I want to be?" "Do I want to live the rest of my life like this?" The answer is usually no, otherwise why would you be asking these questions?

Going through a crisis can happen after a life-changing experience or a traumatic event that makes you question everything in your world. You don't have to be 50 to experience it.

Many marriages will break down because of a midlife crisis and it is usually the man (sorry to be judgemental but that's the truth) who realises that the new car they bought does not make them happy, the new kitchen extension does not make them happy so they try a new partner (leaving the old one behind). It can be quite brutal, and their ex will see it as a moment of madness that they cannot control.

Many people who are going through this will wait it out, accept the situation (as what else can they do?) and see if their spouse or partner comes to their senses and comes back. This is risky as you have to decide how long you are prepared to wait. If this is you, my advice is take this time you have been given to live your own life and find happiness because if you wait you won't be truly happy.

Addictions

Addictions can take many forms and many marriages break up because of them.

Being addicted to sex, porn, gambling, alcohol, drugs and even addictions to game consoles have all been cited in divorce papers.

Clients have told me in the past that their spouse spent more time on the PlayStation than they did with them, or they caught them looking at porn on their laptops when they thought they were asleep.

Addictions in any relationship are hard, especially if the addict does not think they have a problem or does not want help to fix it.

Addictions such as gambling can have disastrous consequences if one person is stealing money out of the joint account to gamble, or takes out big loans to cover gambling debt. It can leave the other person feeling as if they do not trust their partner and leave them wondering, did they every truly know them?

Social Media

I wasn't going to add this, but the rise of social media, Instagram, Facebook and message apps like Messenger and WhatsApp, have sent relationship and marriage breakdowns through the roof! It can become akin to cheating if you are not careful.

People message and chat to people that they like the look of and start to form an emotional attachment to that person, usually because of something that is missing from their current relationship. What starts off as harmless chat, or social media 'likes', can become flirtatious, lead to sexting and before you know it, wham! Your marriage has crumbled.

When I was dating, I had a lot of messages from men on dating apps who were in unhappy relationships and wanted to have some fun. The problem was they didn't tell me straight away, so I got into conversations with them and got to the point of meeting up with them. Then it would transpire that they were still in a marriage or relationship, but they were not happy. Being a victim of infidelity, I was not going to carry on with any man who was still married or in a relationship. My response to them was always, "I don't care if you're George

Clooney, I am not getting involved with a married man. Sort it out with your wife or partner first."

My rule would be, if you're still living under the same roof as them, I'm not interested. I didn't want to be part of a love triangle or break up a marriage or long-term relationship.

I sat listening to a client whose husband had done just that and left the marital home for someone he had met on Facebook. She was absolutely devastated. Did the relationship last? No! But by then, my client didn't want him back as she had moved on. It's a risky business.

Whatever the reasons for your break-up, it will make you question who you are, why you are here and what the rest of your life is going to be like. Yep, it's scary, but one step at a time. Slowly, slowly, catchy monkey.

I went through a huge 'Why?' stage. It consumed my waking thoughts. I did not sleep properly for six months. I was suffering from hypervigilance and could not relax from the thoughts that were in my headspace. It was exhausting and yet, I couldn't sleep. I couldn't relax enough to read and I love reading. If I sat down in the day, I would jump up almost immediately, because I felt guilty for sitting down and had to keep myself busy until the evening in the hope I would be tired enough to sleep. Yes I was exhausted, but still I couldn't sleep. AAARRRGGGHHHH!

It's an awful position to be in. Was this healthy? No. Did it help me? No.

If you are in the middle of the 'Why?' storm, listen to an audio book or relaxing music at night until you fall asleep. You could download a calm app that plays rain or waves to help you relax. This will focus your mind away from automatic and negative thoughts, even if it's just for a while.

Here are some more techniques and tools you could try:

Brain dump – write down all the things that come into your mind, emotions, thoughts, questions and feelings. If you have written this all down, it's not taking up space in your head. And it's still going to be there in the morning.

Meditate – either first thing in the morning or last thing at night. Start slowly at first as the negative thoughts will creep in time and time again until you have learned to push them back and think about what makes you smile or what you are grateful for. Imagining that I am lying on a beach, feeling the sand on my skin and hearing the waves lapping on the shore always works for me.

Start journaling – write down your thoughts, feelings, triumphs and disasters, especially what you are grateful for. This will help you get clarity and help you heal.

There is no right or wrong to how you're feeling, how you will deal with it, and how long it will take to get over. Unfortunately, there is no magic wand to make it all go away.

You will have to accept that it is going to be hard, challenging, and at times you will feel as if you can't take any more.

You will have to learn to accept that this is how you're feeling, and that you have to go through it in order to heal.

It's a really frustrating place to be, as you want to go from broken to healed straight away. You want the pain to stop and you don't want to go through the struggle and challenges that will inevitably arise.

Why? Because, it's going to be hard and who likes hard? Some people never fully recover because they haven't given themselves the time or allowed themselves the space to heal. They may jump headfirst into the first relationship that comes along and be back at square one when it all goes wrong. People who have suffered abuse and trauma can take years to heal, and some never fully recover, but with the right help they can go on to lead fulfilled and happy lives.

Did I get the answers that I wanted after both of my marriage breakdowns? No, not entirely. Do I need or want them now? No. Do I feel as if I want or need an apology? No.

Why is this? Because I realised that getting this would not change the situation. It would not change what had happened. Some people can't move on properly until they have the answers that serve as some form of closure. It's OK to ask your ex for this, but you need to realise that you may not get it.

You deserve to heal; give yourself time to get over your break-up.

Top Tip

Let go of the 'Why?' It will not do you or your mental health any good. Put all your 'Why?' questions on paper (brain dump them). Write a letter to your ex with everything you want to say to them. Then put it away, throw it away or burn it. You may never get the answers you seek and when you do you may not need or want them.

CHAPTER 3

Blame

Don't blame people for disappointing you, blame
yourself for expecting too much.

Anonymous

You know you are single, and you know why, but do you
know who is to blame? Funnily enough, this is the chapter
I wrote last – and to be honest I wasn't sure whether I was
going to include it, but everyone plays the blame game after
a break-up.

Why? Because it makes them feel better and who doesn't like
to feel better after feeling crap?

Are you to blame? Or are you one of the pity party who likes
to play the victim and blames every little thing that happened
on your ex? Have you become locked into a vicious cycle of
being the victim? Everyone loves a victim, don't they?

Before I go any further, the only exception to this is abuse.
Anyone who has suffered any type of abuse in a relationship

is NOT to blame. The blame rests solely on the abuser. Ironically, many victims of abuse blame themselves for the abuse dished out because they have been conditioned to believe that everything is their fault and not the fault of the perpetrator. Many victims of abuse are told: "If you hadn't done this, or said that, I wouldn't have done what I did."

These feelings of 'I am to blame' carry on until the person who has suffered regains control and self-worth and realises that it was not their fault. Even after that, they still blame themselves for getting involved with their abuser in the first place, but maybe that is another book for another time.

It's human nature that when we come out of something awful, we look for something or someone to blame. Someone has to be the scapegoat to allow us to move on easily and feel better about the whole situation and ourselves. We do it to justify what happened and to make sense of the 'Why?'

Who doesn't enjoy playing the blame game with a bunch of friends over a few drinks, putting the world to rights and tarring everyone of the same gender with the same brush? We've all done it, and it felt good, but being totally honest, it's just not as simple as that, is it?

In the cold light of day, do you want to spend your waking hours blaming anything and everything for what happened to you? If you do this, you will never learn anything. You will not begin to accept and learn what part you played in the break-up. You will not be able to fully accept what happened and move forwards.

People will go over their break-up story hundreds if not thousands of times, telling everyone who will listen (willingly or not) how it was all their ex's fault; how they found out that they were cheating or gambling; how they decided to end it because they were sick of the arguments and so on and so on ...

And they will still be telling the same story in years to come because they haven't accepted their portion of blame and they haven't learned the valuable lessons that they needed to.

To blame your ex entirely for what has happened, without putting any blame onto yourself, falls into narcissist territory. Narcissists never blame themselves for the negative things that happen in their lives, ever. They are so full of their own importance that they blame everyone around them so that they don't have to look deep inside to see who they truly are. The only time a narcissist will accept blame is when it is in their best interests to do so and if they gain something that they want from it, whether that be a new love interest, a new job or to make more money.

Narcissists don't lose any sleep over apportioning all the blame onto one person, if it gets them to where they want to be. An example of this is someone who told me that they left their second wife because she was fat, lazy and had high expectations and NOT because he had an affair and had no use for her any more. His current partner fed his ego and gave him the excitement that he wanted. Needless to say she didn't last long either as someone else came to take her place.

So, if you're not a narcissist, where do you fit on the personality scale where blame is concerned? Most of us sit in the middle of the scale, which has emotion at one end and logic at the other. If truth be told, everyone has elements of certain personality disorders, like narcissism or sociopathy, in them. The difference is that many of us can control it and it doesn't affect us or anyone else in the extreme ways that it would with a sociopath, narcissist or someone with another personality disorder.

So, if you fit anywhere within what is considered the 'norm' of the spectrum you will carry a certain amount of blame.

💜 I didn't listen to them.

💜 I didn't try hard enough.

💜 I put my needs before theirs.

💜 I was an awful person.

💜 I didn't take account of their feelings.

💜 I didn't help around the house enough.

💜 I didn't show them enough love.

💜 I wasn't there for them when they needed me most.

💜 I argued over every little thing.

The list can seem endless. If you really think about your break-up, you should be able to blame your actions or choices in part for what happened, however hard that is. No one likes taking the blame but the thing about moving on from a break-up is owning your choices and actions; accepting and acknowledging blame is part of that process.

Shifting blame entirely onto the other person takes away any hope of self-improvement. You know the saying "People in glass houses shouldn't throw stones"?

*When you blame others, you give up your
power to change.*

Dr Robert Anthony

No truer words could be said. There is no change if you don't
know how to change.

If you are blame-free, what is there to change? That would
make you perfect – and nobody's perfect.

This whole book is about change, moving forwards and
learning to be a better person. Don't make the mistake of
thinking that you don't need to blame yourself for any of it,
unless, of course, you are a narcissist! I'm sorry if you feel I
have been harsh, and to be honest you probably didn't need
to hear this at this time, especially if you're struggling to get
through each day, but I never promised that this book was
an easy read. This book will hopefully help you to face some
cold, harsh truths that will enable you to be the person you
were meant to be all along.

Top Tip

*Know what you were to blame for in your break-up.
Apportion it how you like, but learn from it and use it for
self-improvement.*

CHAPTER 4

Mental

Mental health is not a destination but a process. It's about how you drive not where you're going.

Noam Shpancer

Let us talk about your mental health. Whatever the reasons behind your break-up, your mental health is going to take a serious knock. The effects of a break-up or divorce on both your mental and physical health cannot be underestimated; it will manifest itself in ways that you never thought it would.

You will be dealing with so many emotions that you will be in an emotional mess, dealing with automatic negative thoughts. Your confidence and self-worth will have taken a huge blow. That's before anxiety, depression, panic attacks, PTSD (CPTSD), hypervigilance, bipolar and all manner of other more serious mental health issues that can arise. On top of all of that you will be worried about the effects of your break-up on your children and other family members, who will be affected in one way or the other.

Not long after my first marriage breakdown, my then mother-in-law discovered she had terminal cancer and sadly passed away. My parents were obviously very concerned about me and after my second marriage breakdown, my mum became extremely ill. I always wonder if what happened to me, and the stress that she was under, contributed in some way to the onset of her illness.

You will also be worried about your finances. You'll worry about how money and possessions will be split and where (and how) you are going to live. It's probably most worrying if you were a stay-at-home mum who looked after the children while your spouse went to work, or you have to sell the shared house in order to try and fund two separate homes. On top of that, there is maintenance to sort out, solicitors' fees and lots more. Some people stay together until their children are 18 because they cannot afford to split up before then.

I know someone who ended up being sectioned under the Mental Health Act because of their relationship breakdown. It was not a great time for them and it took them months to get to a place where they could function as a 'normal human being'. Mental health issues can be serious and life-threatening, especially when you take into account self-harm, suicidal thoughts, and addictions.

I ended up in hospital days before my first Christmas with my children in my new house after my second marriage breakdown. My body had just decided to give up. I was in agony. I couldn't move (even to get to the toilet) and I had no idea how I was going to make it to Christmas. I actually thought that was it, my life as I knew it was over. The day before had been great, a bit of last-minute Christmas shopping, a catch-up with my girlfriends in the local bar with a couple of drinks –

all was well. I went to bed at around midnight and woke up at 3.00 a.m. in the most unimaginable pain, far more pain than I'd ever experienced before. Even breathing was hard. I lay there for hours. I could not move. I did not want to call my dad in the middle of the night, so I just lay there. I lay there thinking, "Well that's gone and done it, I'll be in hospital all over Christmas or maybe longer."

I lay there thinking that I was going to lose my job and felt pretty annoyed that I had probably lost my social life and everything that came with it. I even thought, "Who is going to want me now? I'm a forty-something women who cannot even get out of bed."

Those few hours from 3.00 a.m. to 7.00 a.m. were the longest hours of my life. I was worried in case my children woke up and saw me in agony. I didn't want to put them through any more than they had already been through.

At the hospital, I was pumped full of steroids and told I could go home for Christmas on the understanding that I rested. "Are you having a laugh?" I thought to myself! I had got my parents, my sister and her husband coming round. But I nodded in agreement as there was no way that I was spending Christmas in hospital and I think they could see how determined I was. I managed to get through Christmas, with help, and I felt OK. I was worried that when the steroids left my body, I would be back to square one, but it never happened, and I was so grateful for that. It was like I'd been given a second chance and a huge warning not to push myself that hard again.

The few months leading up to this hospital emergency had been spent burning the candle at both ends. I had moved into my new house and spent most of my spare time up ladders with a paint brush. I had been living life as a single person (when my children were not with me) and with hindsight it probably wasn't the best thing to do. I had also lived with a chronic disease for most of my adult life and been on a myriad of drugs over the years to keep it at bay, so I wasn't the healthiest of people to begin with.

The body and brain are complicated organs and there are many physical symptoms that can arise when suffering mental health issues. These are immeasurable and can be far-reaching. You can be OK one day and the next you are suffering with stiff joints, rashes, IBS, headaches, sickness, diarrhoea and dizziness. I read somewhere that a woman who had gone through a nasty divorce and mental health issues woke up one morning unable to feel the left-hand side of her body. I am a great believer in physical symptoms being linked in some way to our mental health and our negative and traumatic experiences.

For instance, having depression can lead to severe physical symptoms from fatigue and muscle aches to headaches, vision problems and stomach pain.

Mental health problems can lead to your immune system being compromised and that will leave you open to more coughs, colds, and flu-like symptoms as well as many other illnesses.

A book that I have just bought, and cannot wait to read, is by psychiatrist Bessel van der Kolk and called *The Body Keeps the Score*. It's based on the theory that every traumatic experience that we go through will show up one way or another and have a negative impact on our physical bodies.

A break-up and divorce can surely be classed as a negative experience. The book has been described as one of the most important breakthroughs in mental health in the past 30 years.

Looking after your mental health after a break-up is paramount. Getting the right support is just as important. So many people will go to their GP and be prescribed sleeping pills or anti-depressants and if that's what you need, then I'm not going to stop you. I never took them, just because I was determined that I was going to get on top of this without any more drugs in my system. Yes, I went to see a counsellor (after both my marriage breakdowns). Divorce coaches did not really exist where I lived. I had around six sessions after each break-up and they really did help me to clarify my thoughts and feelings, help me to see a way forwards and to realise that I could turn these experiences into a learning process to be a better person.

So, what can you do if the mental health monster rears its head? And it probably will, even if it's months down the line.

Do not suffer in silence. Please reach out, even if it's just to a friend, so that you can get support. Just a small chat can do the world of good.

Go to your GP if you need to and they will signpost you to get counselling or more specialised help if that's what you need. Don't feel a failure if you are given sleeping pills or anti-depressants as they will help you enormously in the short term.

Exercise as much as you can and get outside. Exercising and being outdoors releases all of those happy endorphins that make you feel great! It's a win-win as you will exercise more because of it.

Practise yoga and/or meditation. This will help your breathing if you're suffering from anxiety and help with calming your mind. This worked wonders for me and stopped me running at 100 miles per hour. I still do both, years later, and I'm totally in tune with my inner hippie.

Practise breathing exercises. There are so many great apps for this and they will help with anxiety and stress levels. One of my favourite breathing techniques is where you inhale through your nose for a count of four, hold for four and then sigh the breath out through your mouth for four. I usually do this to de-stress after a busy day.

Practise gratitude, even if it's just spending a few minutes each day thinking about what you are grateful for and not what you have lost. You don't have to go to the trouble of having a gratitude book or a jar (although if it helps, do it!). Practising gratitude will also help with automatic negative thoughts such as guilt and jealousy. You're less likely to feel guilty about something if you are feeling grateful for something else. So, instead of feeling guilty about your children, feel grateful for having them in the first place.

Surround yourself with positive and energised people as their energy will boost and lift yours. The worst thing you can do is spend time with other people who are suffering mental health issues. It can really bring you down.

I have a friend, who I love dearly but who suffers with bouts of depression. I love the fact that she can talk to me and feel better after it. If I had seen a lot of her during my mental health issues, I think it would have added to my anxiety and made me feel worse. I realise that many of us have suffered with mental health issues and I don't want you to ignore your family and friends because of it. I'm just saying if you are having a very bad time, it may not be in your interests to see a lot of them.

Laugh as much as you can. Laughter is such a simple pleasure and for me, after what seemed like months of crying, it was a revelation to laugh again. Laughing relieves tension, boosts your immune system, and decreases your stress hormones. I loved joking around with my children and friends or watching something funny on TV and still do. Laughter was high on my wish list when I started dating again, which I talk more about in a later chapter.

Think positive thoughts. Your mind will be full of negative thoughts and doubts. The trick to get rid of them is to think about the positive opposite. So instead of thinking, "No one will ever love me again," think to yourself, "Someone will love me again". By doing this you will eventually get rid of the negative thoughts (sometimes not entirely) but if you think positively then you will start to act and live positively.

Do things that make you happy; lots of them, because you can!

Music and dancing were at the top of my happy list. I found a love of music that I didn't have before and spent most of the spare time I had listening to music and dancing around in my new kitchen with or without my children. Let's face it, there are lots of energising songs out there to keep you motivated and invigorated.

> *Sing like no one is listening, love like you never been hurt, dance like no one is watching and live like it is heaven on earth.*
>
> Mark Twain

Top Tip

Be kind to yourself. You have been through a lot and cannot be expected to just return back to your normal self. To be honest, when you are out the other side you won't be the same person, you will be better!

CHAPTER 5

Erase

An ex is an ex for a reason. There's a reason your ex didn't make it to your future.

Anonymous

If only it were that simple. Wouldn't it be great if we could just erase our exes from our lives as if they never existed? This is never going to happen, especially if you have children. Exes are part of your story, whether you like it or not. They are part of your history and how you are going to get to where you need to be.

Your time with your ex may be a huge part of your life that you want to forget about and destroy, but you are never going to erase everything completely. I always look at both my marriages as learning experiences that were necessary to get me to the place that I am today. Obviously, I didn't think like that at the time, when I was in the eye of the storm trying to find a way out and get through each day. If someone had told me five years ago that I would be divorced again, be a divorce coach and writing a book, I would have thought they were nuts! Yet, here we are. If it wasn't for my break-ups, I wouldn't be the strong, determined and happy person that I am now. So for that, I am extremely grateful.

If you do not have children with your ex, lucky you. This part is going to be so much easier. If you do have children, this is going to be bloody hard because you will need to have some form of contact with your ex (maybe for years to come) for the sake of your children. My children were one and six when my marriages broke down, so I had it hardcore. I will talk more about children in a later chapter.

Cut ties on ALL social media

This sounds like common sense, but the amount of people who still look at their ex's Facebook posts or Instagram pictures to see what they are up to, and who with, baffles me. It's akin to torture. I had a client who was in bits because they had seen a Facebook post of their ex on a boys' holiday. She was visualising all the women he was going to meet and hook up with and it was keeping her awake at night.

I sat with her as she 'unfriended' him and deleted all of the social media that still tied her to her ex. She felt as if she was losing control, but I reminded her that by doing this she would be in control of herself (not her ex, as he can't be controlled). He was an ex, so why would she put herself through this misery? I told her to focus on her life and make it so fulfilling that she wouldn't need to lie awake at night, thinking about what her ex was up to.

Remember, your ex's life is their life to live and you have to live yours.

Depersonalise your ex

The best thing you will ever do to start healing is to refer to your ex by their initial or give them a nickname. So, P for Peter and J for Jane. When they crop up in conversation (as they will, lots to begin with), it makes it much easier to call them by their initial or nickname. It depersonalises them and makes them less significant in your life. They are your ex, so why would you call them by their full name? I even suggest that people use initials or a nickname on their phones as well.

When they crop up in conversations, you can say things like, "Yes, I saw T out shopping yesterday," or "I called S about having the children at the weekend."

It will feel really odd to begin with (as if they are a different person) and some people don't feel comfortable with it, but if your persevere, you will start thinking about them in a less significant way and even start to think of them by their nickname or initial in your head.

Be careful when using nicknames though. I know someone who had their ex-wife in their phone as 'The B@tch'. He had clearly not dealt with his divorce in the right way and not fully healed. And you wouldn't want your children to find out about that.

Negative to positive

This next exercise is very empowering. It allows you to start thinking about the positive side of a negative and start to see your future without your ex in it.

What you do is list all of the things that you are not going to miss about your ex, followed by the positive in the situation. For example:

I will not miss my ex's snoring.

Followed by:

I will get an uninterrupted and peaceful night's sleep (Sounds great doesn't it?).

Or:

I will not miss having to watch EastEnders.

Followed by:

I can now watch what I want to on TV.

You can write as many things as you want and you start to see all of the positive things about being without your ex. It's a win-win.

Dialling down thoughts

Try and limit the number of times that you think about your ex and what has happened. Of course, to begin with, it will be all that you think about.

When you start thinking about your ex, try to do something constructive that will help take your mind off them. If you are constantly thinking about them, to the point of not being able to do anything else, try spending ten minutes just thinking about them, thinking about what has happened and how you feel. Yes, it's going to be difficult but face these feelings head-on and accept them. After ten minutes, say to yourself, "I can think about something else now", knowing that you can think about them later on, or the next day. Over time, these thoughts will become less and less. Don't try and push them down. In order to heal and move forwards, you need to allow yourself to break the emotional ties that are still there.

One of my clients was struggling because his ex-wife had a new partner who was starting to stop at their old house overnight. How did he know this? I hear you say. It was because the ex had told him. They were on very friendly terms and would talk about how things were going most days. This is tricky territory to be in. When he told me about this, I was screaming inside at him, "Why are you so close to her, she's an ex for a reason?" I didn't tell him outright that it wasn't a good idea, as he could see no harm in it. I knew it was because he couldn't let go and deep down wanted to see if things would change. But for the most part, it crucified him inside knowing that his ex's new boyfriend was staying over at the house that they used to live in together and where his children still lived. He got so obsessed with this new boyfriend that he would drive to the house and see if his car was still parked outside in the morning, which it usually was. Being party to your ex's every move is not healthy and can lead to obsessive behaviour. All I can say is that it didn't do him any good in the long run.

Mind movies

This is a great technique if you are worried or anxious about bumping into your ex, when you haven't seen them in a while, even more so if they might be with their new partner (ouch!). 'Mind movies' is exactly what it says. Firstly, play through an imaginary scenario in your head where you bump into your ex (with or without their new partner). Go with your instinct and play through what would happen. You may burst into tears, get into an intense conversation over what happened, get angry, hurl a few insults or cross over the road and pretend you didn't see them.

It's OK whatever happens, because it's only in your head. Now, think about what you would like to be able to do: not cross the road or get into a conversation but hold your head up high, give them a nod or say hello and walk on proudly. Play this scenario in your head for as many times as you want and keep practising it on a regular basis. When you do bump into your ex, you will know exactly what you have to do, and it will feel like you are playing the movie in real time.

Visualisation

Spend time each day visualising how you want your life to be in the future (without your ex in it, obviously). Visualise how happy you are going to be, how content you will be. What are you doing? Who are your with? Where do you live? All of these thoughts will help you to feel more at peace with your situation and you will start to feel more in control, stronger and more determined to move forwards. Make a vision board, or vision journal, and then you can add to it when you feel inspired and look at it when you feel yourself slipping backwards.

Top Tip

Change your mindset. Thinking about your ex will not change that they are an ex. So, why waste time thinking about them? Thinking about them will not change what has happened so why give them room in your headspace?

CHAPTER 6

Support

Good friends help you find important things when you have lost them .... Things like your smile, your hope and your courage.

Doe Zantamata

'Support'. I cannot say this word enough times. This is the most fundamental thing when you are going through a break-up, separation or divorce. You wouldn't go into an exam without doing all of your revision. You wouldn't do a bungee jump until you had had all of your safety checks (as well as a stiff drink) and completed your safety training. So why would you go through a divorce or separation without knowing who, or what, are part of your support network?

Here is my guide to setting up a support network.

You will need:

A very close friend

I've deliberately not said family member, unless your closest friend happens to be your sister or brother. This person is there so that you can cry, vent and get angry, call them at any hour, drink wine with them, and they can just be there to be your emotional punchbag (not literally). If they are a good friend they will understand and support you.

You will find that you lose friends after a break-up. In the beginning everyone and their dog will be offering support and help and a shoulder to cry on, even if you aren't close friends. It's human nature to reach out to others in crisis, but losing friends (especially friends that you had together) is normal. Some friends will drop off because they do not know how to support you. You find out very quickly who your true friends are. My closest friend during both my break-ups came round in the middle of the night once when I was having a particularly bad time. I often joke to her that I can never break our friendship as she knows far too much about me!

An exercise buddy

This can be a friend, family member, colleague, neighbour or someone you meet at the gym.

Keeping active is very important when getting over a break-up or going through a divorce, even if it's just someone to walk the dog with. Getting outdoors is vital to lifting your mood and feeling energised.

Emotions like anger can bubble up from nowhere. You will have excess energy to use up or you may explode when you least expect it. If you are suffering from hypervigilance, or running on adrenaline, you will find it very difficult to sit still or relax. You will need an outlet for these energy bursts. I used to walk, sometimes miles, each day. I would park my car up and just go, not knowing where I was going or how long it would take. Yes, it was a little reckless, especially when I had the school pick-up to do in the afternoon. I also swam (great for thinking and clearing your head) and started to practise yoga. I also did a few boxing classes and went to the gym with a friend. Some people can get addicted to exercise; it's like a drug. They try to fill up on the highs they feel when they are exercising and also try to block out what has happened. It's also a way of filling up all of the spare time they now have.

Legal advice

This sounds like common sense, but so many people do not seek financial or legal advice, especially at the very beginning. Knowing what you are entitled to, and how the divorce process works, is going to help you focus on what needs to be done and when. Lots of solicitors offer free, initial consultations. It's imperative that you ask lots of questions and feel comfortable with your solicitor.

I had two very different experiences with both of my divorces.

I appointed a solicitor for my first divorce as I didn't know what the hell I was doing, partly due to the fact that I started divorce proceedings very quickly. I knew that our marriage was not going to be saved, so why wait?

My solicitor gave me great advice and guided me to make the right decisions. Mainly, not going down the adultery route but citing unreasonable behaviour. She was a calm influence when I was struggling to keep my head above water.

My second divorce was done painlessly, following a two-year separation and all through letters. This is a good route to take if finances and child custody arrangements have already been agreed.

The 'no-fault' divorce bill is just being passed at this moment. I think it will help enormously for all couples to have the option of a divorce that is as pain-free and blame-free as possible.

A coach or counsellor

Counsellors and coaches are different, so do your homework beforehand and find out what it is you need help with. Coaches and counsellors will specialise in certain things, usually because they have been through them themselves. It's worth checking this before you book a session with them.

What is the difference between a coach and a counsellor?

Counsellors usually deal with past traumas like abuse, childhood trauma and past events that have had a great impact on your life, such as the death of a close family member. They are trained to listen and help you find a way through your problems in order for you to come to your own answers. They will not offer advice, but they do offer a safe and confidential space to talk about things that have happened in your life.

Coaches are more proactive and will help you with the here and now. They will help you set targets and goals in order for you to get the most out of your life. Many coaches, like me, will also offer counselling and vice versa. Most of the clients I see as a divorce coach need someone to listen to what has happened to them and they need someone to empathise, which is a large part of what counsellors do.

A point to note is that both counselling and coaching are not regulated, and anyone can set themselves up as a counsellor or coach. Before hiring someone, check to see what professional body they are registered with, or what course they took to gain a certification.

Top Tip

Draft up your support network as soon as you are able. It is not set in stone and can be changed as your needs change.

CHAPTER 7

Time

Time doesn't heal emotional pain; you have to learn how to let go.

Roy T Bennett

Time is that elusive entity that cannot be controlled. So many people going through a break-up will say, 'If only I could turn back time, I'd do this, say that, change this'.

But what's happened has happened. It cannot be changed. It's so easy to dwell on the 'what ifs?'.

Yes, it is a cliché and people will tell you that time is a great healer. I'm not going to tell you any different. However, you cannot let time take over. You need to help time along, kick it up the backside if you need to, but don't let time take its course or you may find that you're in the same place in years to come.

I know people who still feel the same, have the same issues and still feel aggrieved over their past relationship and what happened years afterwards, because they have not dealt with it in the correct way.

What you do need to do is give yourself time to grieve. This seems so simple, but many people miss this step. They may shed a few tears but they do not give this part of the process the time it deserves. They feel they have to be very British and carry on as if nothing has happened, or they fill the space left by their ex with someone or something else and miss the process out completely. This is a very impulsive thing to do as at some point it will come back and smack you between the eyes if you have not dealt with it. Grieve for the end of your relationship or marriage. Grieve for the person you were as half of a couple, grieve for the loss of everything that you thought was safe, grieve for the loss of what you thought your future was.

I coached a man who was struggling with his marriage breakdown. He was waiting for his divorce to come through and had moved into his own flat, but he was spiralling into depression and using drink as a way through. He had not cried. He wouldn't and couldn't allow himself this one human emotion.

I asked myself why this was. Many people will stuff their feelings down and use alcohol, drugs, partying or promiscuity to block out their feelings of grief or sadness.

Did he feel as if crying would make him weak? Did he feel as if crying would compromise his masculinity? After a few sessions skirting around the subject, I got to the stage where I felt he was ready to answer the question and I felt that enough trust had been built for me to be able to ask him. After some hesitation, he replied that if he allowed himself to cry then he would go past the point of no return and not be able to get back. He was scared; scared to allow his emotions out for fear of them completely overwhelming him. I explained to him that if he held on to these emotions, then they would consume him in every which way possible. I asked him to give himself permission to cry and if his feelings did overwhelm him, then let them, as he needed to release the emotion. Even if he spent all day in bed crying, he would have moved a step closer to acceptance and healing.

When grieving, in order to start healing, you have to accept and own your feelings however difficult that is to do. Admit that the feelings hurt, admit that it is hard and that you feel like shit. Admit all of the negative emotions like anger and shame. When you face your feelings head-on and allow yourself to feel them, it can feel like a huge release and be extremely cathartic.

You don't have to do 'a Bridget Jones' and spend all day in bed with a box of tissues, eating ice cream (well, you can if that's what you want to do). But you should allow yourself to feel sad, messed up, lonely and heartbroken. The process of healing is fraught with pain, difficulty, sadness and challenges, but when you come out the other side, you will feel a new and much better person for it.

Many clients will often ask me how long it takes to get to get over a divorce and reach a place of acceptance and happiness. I can't answer them. Everyone is different; everyone takes their own path, at their own pace. Some people take a few months and others take years, but if you are proactive and don't let time rule you, you will get to the winning post much quicker and that is always a good thing!

Top Tip

Make time your greatest superpower – stop it if you need to tread water and speed it up if you are ready to make huge changes.

CHAPTER 8

Children

Teach your daughters to grow up into strong, independent women, and teach your sons how to treat one.

Anonymous

I'm not going to lie, if you don't have children with your ex, your life is going to be so much easier. You will probably skip this chapter and I don't blame you. You can carry on with your life and not have to communicate or see your ex on a regular basis. If, like me, you do have children, this is not going to be easy. To a certain extent you have to put your children's wants and needs to the top of the list of your priorities, especially at the beginning, because they need to feel loved, cared for, secure and safe whatever age they are. For most parents, the guilt we will carry for our children will be immense.

My children gave me the strength to carry on each day, knowing that they needed me. They gave me hope. They made me smile each day when all I wanted to do was cry.

They stopped me from doing the most selfish thing a person could ever do (I think you know what I'm talking about here). I'm not saying that I was the model parent. I'm not saying that they didn't see me cry or get upset or have a full-blown panic attack. And for that I felt deeply ashamed.

When I got married for the second time, I vowed to myself that my son would not go through what my daughter did but yep, it happened again and was far worse. I carried that guilt for a long time – still do to a certain extent. What I do know is that they are both happy and loved children. Of course, they ask questions, even now. On the way to school, my son will sometimes ask why me and his dad split up and I try and answer him, although telling your children the whole truth is not always a good idea. As they grow up they will start to fit pieces together and understand. My daughter now has a better understanding of what happened and holds no grudge and does not apportion blame to me or her dad.

I always think about a poem called "This Be the Verse" by Philip Larkin that goes: "They fuck you up, your mum and dad. They may not mean to, but they do. They fill you with the faults they had and add some extra, just for you."

It ends with the line:

"Get out as early as you can, and don't have any kids yourself!"

When there are children involved, you will have wobbles. You will say and do things in front of your children that you will later regret. It's human nature. Of course, common sense tells you not to use your children as a weapon to hurt your ex, but it occasionally happens, either subconsciously or not, when there is a lot of hurt and anger. And if you do, you will regret it months or years down the line. Emotions around your children will be high (I was, and still am, very protective of both my children – although my stroppy teenage daughter can, and does, look after herself. I'm not sure where she gets it from!) so please try not to let your feelings or emotions overshadow what your children need from you as parents.

I remember taking my daughter to her dad's new flat. He had just come back from a boys' holiday and I was excited to tell him about our daughter's potty training efforts and what he needed to do as she was staying with him for the day. Armed with daughter, potty and bags, I rang the bell and was told I couldn't come inside as he already had someone there. I was cross at this and proceeded to put my daughter and her things back in the car and drive home. I was cross because he hadn't seen his daughter for over a week, and I wanted to tell him about how far she had come. As I wasn't going to be invited in to meet his new partner, I didn't feel that I wanted to leave our daughter with him and his new partner either. Looking back, it was probably an overreaction, and like I said, emotions can take over. But I thought I was doing what was best for her when in reality I wasn't. I'm sure she wouldn't have cared if someone else was there, she was only two. But I wanted her to have time with her dad and couldn't see why he would want his new partner there as well. I realised after that, that I wanted my daughter to be happy and seeing her dad on a regular basis, regardless of whether he was with his new partner or not.

I totally understand if your children do not see their other parent due to a court order, a custodial sentence or something similar. It is not uncommon for one parent to just abandon their children and move on, sometimes to another country. This happens more than we realise. If you're in this situation, you are going to have to find your inner lion and summon up the courage and strength to parent alone. I take my hat off to you.

At the beginning, whenever I went to drop my son off at his dad's (we had already agreed on custody arrangements without having to go through the courts and if you can do this it will be easier, cheaper and better for your mental health) I wanted to figuratively slap my ex (I never did, can I just add) because I didn't agree with him moving his new partner into the marital home as soon as I had moved out. In my eyes, my son was getting used to living in two houses and also getting used to having parents that lived apart. Now he also had to adapt to a new partner and other children in his home. I had to be extremely strong when I dropped him off and smile, wave and give him a kiss. All I wanted to do was ask my ex, "Why have you done this? Why aren't you letting him settle first? Why are you being selfish and just thinking about yourself?"

I was told when I questioned this new arrangement that it was nothing to do with me. So, I learned very quickly that I couldn't control what happened when he wasn't with me and to a certain extent you have to let it go. I know it's hard.

The most important thing to do is talk to your children, reassure them that you both love them, answer any questions they may have if you can and at a level that they understand. Obviously, you are not going to tell them things that they are not old enough to understand, and to be honest this will serve no purpose and won't contribute to your child's happiness. I remember telling my son that Mummy and Daddy had been very unhappy and now that we lived in different houses we were both much happier. I also did the whole spiel of two houses, two birthdays, two Christmases, etc., which made both my children very happy!

Even though you are not telling the whole truth about your situation, children are very good at forming their own opinions and as they grow up they will fit the pieces together in their own way and at their own pace. If your children are very young, they will not be able to communicate their feelings and it may show in their behaviour. Aggression, biting, bedwetting and screaming are common.

My first marriage broke down when my daughter was one. She would ask over and over again, 'Where Dadda?' She would cry when I told her that he wasn't here, but she would see him soon. She started to sleep in my bed after just having her own 'big girl' bed. My son did this also. He didn't leave my bed for over a year (my daughter the same). His excuse was that he didn't want me to be lonely, but I know that it was for comfort and I also know that he needed to feel safe. I didn't feel overly guilty about it as I wanted to make sure that I gave my children the emotional support that they needed and deserved.

Any decision you make for your children, as a newly-single parent, you will analyse to the nth degree and second guess whether you are doing the right thing for them. Try not to. Be kind to yourself. Children are resilient and things do not last forever. You may find that your children regress socially and emotionally. They may go back to wearing nappies if they are young, or they may want you to read them a bedtime story when you haven't done it for years. It's their way of coping; they want to be nurtured, loved and to feel safe.

Even if it was your decision to leave your partner, co-parenting is tricky, and you will have to keep your ex in the loop and make certain decisions together. Again, this is very difficult if you have different parenting styles or you don't agree on things like where they should go to school or what is the best bedtime.

The hardest part is letting go of control when they are at the other parent's place. Decisions will be made without you, and to be honest, sometimes it's best not to know. Knowing that your child was taken on a shopping trip when they were ill and off school does not help. Children have a knack of telling you things like: "I was allowed to eat sweets before bedtime" or "I was told that I didn't have to do my homework if I didn't want to" or "I was allowed to eat meat" when you have brought them up as a strict vegetarian. But let it go!!

For me, it was hard losing control, but I had to tell myself, "Why fight over something or get cross about something that has already happened?" As long as my children were safe and happy, why would I rock the boat? There are exceptions to this rule, and you will have to pick and choose your battles wisely.

I remember picking up my son from school after he had been at his dad's the night before and looking aghast at the star that had been shaved into the side of his head. I remember mouthing "Sorry" to his teacher, as I didn't want her to think that it was my doing. I didn't know whether to laugh, cry or demand to know how and why his dad had allowed it. Inside I was fuming. My son was 8 not 18! I asked my son about his new haircut and he proudly told me that he had wanted a Bethlehem star for Christmas (it was December). I didn't like to tell him that actually he looked like a convict. I just smiled and told him it looked lovely ... but maybe it wasn't school uniform. When I saw his dad next, I thanked him for taking our son to the hairdressers. I think the sarcasm wasn't lost on my ex, but I tried to keep it light.

Accept that you do not have control of your children when they are at your ex's.

Set boundaries at the beginning for what you will and will not accept as regards to your children. Obviously your ex may not abide by these boundaries, but at least you have verbalised them. Keep set days and times for picking up and dropping off and try to make these the 'norm' for your children. Children like routine.

Your ex can disagree (that's their prerogative), they can make things difficult and they can bend the boundaries, but that's not your fault. Over time things do and will change. You will find that you can work together to co-parent your children in a way that suits you both even if it's by email or text only. You will find something that works.

As you will know by now, I am writing this book during the COVID-19 lockdown. My children are spending a week at their dads' and a week at mine instead of having to arrange two lots of drop-offs and pick-ups while they are not at school. It makes it easier and helps to stop the spread of the infection. I set out beforehand that I wanted consistency in respect of schoolwork and bedtimes in the week. Is it being done? I'm not sure.

It seems to be working well and even though I am missing my children, as usually I have them the majority of the time, I am making the most of my child-free weeks.

On the other side of the coin, I know of a women who has had a very nasty email from her ex stating that she needs to buck up her ideas and homeschool them correctly and that he doesn't want to have to pick up the slack!

This sort of demeaning communication does not help anyone, let alone the children involved. It's just point-scoring at its finest by making the other parent feel inferior.

To be honest, if I had received this email I would have emailed to ask him to support his ex-wife more instead of accusing her of sitting on her lazy behind all day (his words not mine) and gone on to let him know what an amazing role model he is being to his children. I know, I can get on my high horse about things at times.

Step-parents

I felt that step-parents and new partners needed their own section because eventually your children may have a new step-parent or a new partner to get to know. Introducing a new partner or step-parent into your child's life can be tricky and needs to be dealt with sensibly and sensitively. Your children have been used to having you all to themselves and now there is someone new in your life. They may worry about what to call the new person, especially if they are going to be a step-mum or step-dad. They may not fully understand what a step-parent means or feel pushed out of this new unit when they are with you. They may feel jealous, sad, angry or anxious and again show their emotions in a negative way or regress.

Both of my experiences with my children are completely different. Even though I have a partner, I still live alone with my children and my partner lives in his house. It's still early days and I would not want to upset the balance of my small family unit by moving my partner in at this time (he both respects this and understands). But both of my children have step-mums.

My daughter, because of the age she was, does not remember me and her dad being married or living together. She has only known her dad and step-mum and her step-dad who was my second husband and the dad of my son. She finds it funny that me and her dad were married and will often laugh about it.

Her relationship with her step-mum is very good. As the youngest and only girl in her dad's house, with two step-brothers, she loved getting all the attention and I think her step-mum loved having another girl in a house full of men! She can talk to her step-mum about things and her step-mum was always on hand to pick her up from school and take her to doctors' appointments when I couldn't. I know they often have girlie nights in when her dad is away. Am I jealous? No, not at all as I know that I am her mum and her step-mum has always been very respectful of that. I also know that my daughter sees me as her best friend and that is the greatest gift that I can have. I'm not saying there have never been difficulties, especially in the beginning when I found out she was the woman that he left me for, but I couldn't have wished for a better step-mum for my daughter.

My son's experience has been totally different because of age and circumstance. My son was six when my marriage to his dad broke down. He had to move to a new house with me and also get used to a new woman being in his dad's life at the same time. He struggled with the huge amount of changes that were happening. He would often say that he wanted his dad to be on his own.

He also struggled when he was told that they were getting married. He became very clingy and anxious, even to the point of having a meltdown over having to call her mum. I had to explain that he didn't have to call her mum if he didn't want to. I was his mum and that wasn't going to change. He also went through a stage of asking me if I was his real mum and wanted me to explain how I knew this. This was a very tricky situation to be in with a nine-year-old boy who hadn't had sex education at school yet. But I tried to explain, as best as I could, and he seemed happy with my explanation – although he couldn't understand why people had babies together who weren't married and so another conversation ensued. We had some very in-depth conversations about things, usually in the car on the way to school or before bedtime as he still loved me to tuck him in. I would reassure him that even though things at his dad's were changing, we still loved him and to speak to his dad about it as well.

It wasn't all plain sailing, though. At one point he had a total breakdown saying that he didn't want to go to the wedding. Hearing this from my son was extremely upsetting and I wasn't in a position at that time to speak to his dad about it. If things had carried on, then yes, I would have done. This situation wasn't ideal, and I'd advise any parent to talk to their ex about things like this if at all possible.

Letting go of your children and having to share them with your ex is hard and painful. When they were born, you would never have thought that you would be in this situation. I know that I certainly didn't, and I definitely didn't think that lightning would strike twice!

The first Christmas with my daughter as a single mum was so special. Even though I felt it when she went to her dad's to have another Christmas with his new family.

I felt the same with my son, but was more used to having to share my children by that time. I mainly felt guilt. I couldn't supply a ready-made new family like their dads had. With me, it was just me. I didn't have a new partner or a new family. Organising the first Christmases and birthdays can be a minefield, but both my exes were happy to let me have the first Christmas with both my children and we now alternate each year. They get two celebrations and what child doesn't like to milk and take full advantage of that, whatever age they are?

Instead of twiddling my thumbs when I didn't have my children (I arranged it with a lot of juggling that they were at their dads' at the same time) I would go for a walk, a swim or a yoga class. I would catch up with friends and make the most of my free nights by going out and staying out sometimes. I began to see my child-free time as 'my time' and began to love it.

When my son announced that he was going to go on holiday with his dad for a week, my first thought was, "Oooh, I can plan a whole week of things to do!" because I arranged for my daughter to be at her dad's at the same time. This system does not always work. When I want a cheeky weekend away, I have to check with both dads and get an OK before I can book anything, and even then, it can all go horribly wrong at the last minute.

Getting to this stage takes time and you will go through feelings of loss, jealousy, frustration, loneliness and lots more! You have to embrace being without your children as much as being with them. It's odd because when my children are at their dads, I don't hear a peep from them unless it is an emergency. They are used to switching from one household to another and the different dynamics in each place. When my children are with me, we are our own little family unit. We are very close and laugh, have fun, dance in the kitchen and talk like any other family as well as annoy the hell out of each other. They know that they can talk to me about anything and that makes me feel as if I am doing a good job. Having a teenage daughter and a nearly teenage son can be challenging at times, but we all know that we love each other and have each other's backs. Our first holiday abroad together was so special, and I am looking forward to the next one.

Having a new partner and introducing them to my children, after being on my own for a year or two, has worked out better than I thought and that is because we took it slowly. My daughter loves the fact that I have finally found someone who she feels is right for me. She likes the fact that I am happy and not dating random men any more (her words). My son felt slightly different. He got a little jealous of the new man in my life and he wanted Mum all to himself. He didn't see why Mum wanted or needed to have a boyfriend. I remember many nights spent on the sofa with my son in between me and my partner while watching a film. It makes me laugh now. My partner has been totally respectful of my situation and would even ask permission if he could give me a kiss in the early days, even if my son said, "No!" He also spoke to my son to reassure him that he wasn't here to take Mum away from him and told him that he was still the most important man in my life, which my son loved! Yes, we don't live together but I'm in no rush. Plus, I like my own space and space to be with my children just on our own.

What I'm saying is, harmony can be achieved over time and you will look back in years to come knowing that you did the right thing by your children.

I am not ashamed to say that I am very protective of them (have I said that already?) and that is because of the guilt that I still feel now and again for not being able to give them the family life that I had. But I know that they are much better off with both a mum and dad that are happy and settled, even though they don't live together.

My daughter took on the role of a second mum to her brother and they make no bones of the fact that they love each other when they aren't annoying each other or pushing each other's buttons.

I know that one day I will have to let them go to navigate their own paths and I'm OK with that. I want them to be happy and fulfilled, knowing that I am there when they need me, and I have great plans for when they have flown the nest .... Something along the lines of going on a road trip and yoga in India!

Top Tip

Push yourself to be the better person, however hard that is. Your ex may have cheated, lied and betrayed you but what's done is done and it's not your children's fault.

Choose your battles wisely. You don't want to be arguing over everything that you don't agree with; save it for when you really need to.

CHAPTER 9

Love

When you are broken, your pieces do not fit back together the same way. When you are fully healed you may be different, but you will be more beautiful and original than before.

Alison Davies, The Little Book of Happiness

Let's face it, when you become single, you don't like yourself, let alone love yourself. You don't feel as if you deserve to love yourself or be happy. You feel guilt, shame, failure and a whole lot of other emotions, massed in a black ball that sits at your core. Learning to love yourself again is one of the most difficult lessons to learn. It's easier to hate ourselves or even flog ourselves daily for what has happened because we feel that we deserve it.

What if I tell you that you deserve to be happy, you deserve to love yourself again, you deserve to have and live the life that you want?

What I do know is that there is no way that you can love anyone else until you love yourself.

How do you go about it? Again, this takes time, work and a lot of self-belief.

Many of us hold on to negative and limiting beliefs about ourselves. These beliefs are formed in childhood and what we do as we grow up is stack up evidence to support these beliefs, making us believe that they are true.

So, it may be that you feel that you are not good enough.

This belief would have been planted in childhood from an event that is deep in your subconscious. It may have been a small thing that made you feel this negative emotion. As you have grown into an adult, other experiences have backed up this belief. Maybe you were told by a sibling or friend that you were not good enough to be on the swimming team, or a teacher had told you to do your work again as it was not up to scratch? You will have stored all of these as evidence to uphold the negative belief that you have. Going through a separation or divorce will certainly bring all of those negative beliefs back, as well as ones like:

♥ I am not loveable.

♥ I am a bad person.

♥ I am not attractive.

♥ I am overweight.

♥ I won't find anyone for me.

The thing you have to do is to trick your brain into believing something different that is opposite to your negative belief of yourself. So, if it's "No one will love me again" you need to turn it into: "Someone will love me again".

The first thing I tell clients to do each day is to look in the mirror and say three positive things about themselves. For example:

💜 I am a good person.

💜 I am strong.

💜 I am funny.

When you are comfortable with saying these things, choose another three things, and so on. I always used to, and still do, practise affirmations when driving.

If you are struggling with a total lack of confidence (which comes with the territory) ask your closest friends and family to write down positive words that describe you and stick them somewhere visible like the fridge or the back of the toilet door. You can't escape them then.

I used to have trouble saying anything good about myself as I didn't feel that I was good enough. For a long time, I couldn't accept compliments and would always bat them back to the person saying them, or I would laugh as if they were totally crazy and couldn't possibly be talking about me. If this is you then I can fully empathise. Getting divorced can have that effect.

The trick is, once you start to say it you will gradually start to believe it. I can remember sitting in a pub in Camden (I'd come away for the weekend with one of my male friends, and yes it was great to be able to have male friends without having to justify it to anyone) and we were talking about our journeys and experiences. He was a great believer in cause and effect and told me that I didn't have enough confidence in my abilities, and I needed to believe that I was a good person. I fully understood where he was coming from, but believing it was proving difficult. I couldn't see why I was a good person and why I deserved happiness. Anyway, after a few drinks I pushed myself through the crowds to go to the toilets that were covered in graffiti (it was quite a rough pub). When I closed the cubicle door and sat down, on the door was some graffiti that said, "You are beautiful, strong and brave". I couldn't quite believe my eyes as there was no other graffiti in this cubicle – odd, I know. When I told my friend what I had seen, he smiled and said it was meant for me to read. I have always carried this little message on my phone since that day. Whenever I was having a bad day, I would look at it.

It took me a long time to love myself. It hampered me having any sort of serious relationship for a long time as I didn't feel that I was worthy of having one. I would push people away because I didn't feel good enough to have someone special. The problem was that I didn't consciously do it, it just happened. I became aware that I was doing it but couldn't help it. I accepted that it was just the way that I was. I was flawed and that's how my life would be. Little by little I began to see my worth. This came from me getting stronger and knowing what I wanted from my life. I became a totally different person to the person I had been during my marriage. I started to believe people when they told me that I was a good and nice person.

Over time, you will start to feel more confident, have more self-worth, begin to like who you are and become able to accept compliments when they are given.

Top Tip

Have a bank of quotes and affirmations that strike a chord with you to get you through bad days or days when you just need a lift.

Keep telling yourself, "I don't have to love someone else to prove that I love myself".

CHAPTER 10

Change

If we don't change, we don't grow. If we don't really grow, we aren't really living.

Gail Sheehy

Making changes is not about cutting off your hair, turning vegan and going to live a simpler life in the forest – well, it could be if that's what you want to do. Usually, it's all about doing things differently as a single person. It's about taking back control of your life and making decisions for yourself. Making changes, however small, will help you to feel more empowered, to be in control of the path ahead of you.

Many people who find themselves single are fearful of change. They have just been through a huge life-changing event and see change as the enemy. They don't want change, they want normality, they want safety, they want the same 'day in, day out' because it's what they know.

Well, the stark reality is that everything in your life has changed. When you're in the eye of the storm, and things are out of your control, the plane is crashing and there is no way to stop it. Yes it's a scary, anxious and lonely place to be, but you can stop the plane crashing and burning if you start to take back control even if it's just small changes. These can lead to enormous ones.

Moving forwards and bringing about change is part of the recovery process. Knowing that the world is not going to come crashing down when you go a different way to work, or cook something that you have never cooked before, can be liberating and lead to bigger changes.

One of the first changes I made when I eventually moved into my new house, apart from decorating every single room (I've nearly finished), was cooking what I wanted to cook. My ex was a very fussy eater and I used to get quite anxious when cooking for him as he would only eat certain things.

Doing my first supermarket shop was odd because I was only shopping for me and my children, but it was highly enjoyable. I took my time and picked things up, thought about what I would like to cook with them and ended up getting quite excited about getting the ingredients to make a goat's cheese risotto.

I say to my clients that even the smallest of steps can turn into the largest of leaps.

To help you to start making small changes, I have devised an exercise that you can complete when you feel ready. It's called 'Taking Steps', obviously!

To make the exercise easier, I've split things up into sections (more like a life coaching wheel) so that you can start to make changes from every section. This is not an extensive list or a compulsory one.

Feel free to make notes under each section of things that you would like to change, or add in steps that I haven't mentioned. Some of the large steps require money and, when you're getting divorced, money is a luxury that some of us do not have. That's OK. Even the small steps will make a difference. I apologise if you feel you are being told how to suck eggs and have heard it all before, but sometimes we need someone else to tell us. Sometimes we need clarification that it's OK to make these changes. Sometimes when we're out of a relationship and going through the awful, gut-wrenching process of separation or divorce, we don't trust ourselves to make the right decisions. Let's face it, we married, or decided to be in a relationship with someone, which didn't last. Why would we trust our own judgement?

Try the exercise over the page.

'TAKING STEPS' EXERCISE

Your physical self
Small steps

Get a new hair style.

Start exercising, whether that is walking, yoga or running.

Eat more healthily. It's true that what you eat helps with both your physical and emotional well-being. Even if you just cut down on junk food and takeaways, or have meat-free days, you're taking steps.

....

....

....

....

....

....

Big steps

Lose weight. (This is easy; everyone loses weight on the divorce diet.)

Join a gym.

Have your teeth done or some cosmetic surgery. Yes, this is radical, but some people do. I thought about getting my teeth straightened at one point, as I went through a phase where I felt that I needed to be perfect, but I'm a rebellious sort and thought, "Sod it! Love me, love my crooked teeth!"

....

....

....

....

....

Your emotional self

Small steps

Daily meditation. Find somewhere quiet, sit in a comfortable position, whether that be on a chair or cross-legged on the floor, and give it a go – even if it's just for five minutes. If you're struggling, download a meditation app.

Practise daily gratitude. Writing a list is always good. What has gone well today? What have your enjoyed or learned?

Talk or vent to a friend. Obviously there should be plenty of alcohol involved.

Reads lots of books on divorce. You've got that covered! Read self-help books; knowledge really is power.

....

....

....

....

....

Big steps

Join a meditation group. Buddhist centres are great for this. You don't have to pay, and they welcome you like lost children.

See a counsellor or a life coach. Obviously.

Go on a retreat. One in a hot country will do nicely. I took myself off on a yoga retreat in Mallorca. It was a defining moment for me as I had to prove to myself that I could do it. It made me realise that I could do it and I had the most amazing time. I was supposed to be going on a divorce retreat in England but as you already know I'm rebellious and said "Sod it! I want to lie on a sun lounger and swim in the sea." I came home feeling empowered, wanting to carry on my yoga journey. I also started internet dating because I met a couple there who had met on Match.com and had just moved in together. Just saying ....

....

....

....

....

....

....

Your friendships

Small steps

See your friends more. This is common sense to most single people, but actually hard to do when your friends still have marriages and relationships to nurture or have small children.

But, even if it's just asking if they want to catch up over a quick coffee (baby in tow) or go and see a film at the cinema, they can only say no, and if they do, arrange another date.

If you have work colleagues, arrange an informal after-work drink. They may not be your friends in the true sense of the word, but it is the next step to a social life.

....

....

....

....

....

....

Big steps

Have a complete friendship overhaul. Yes, brutal, I know, but when you go through a break-up or divorce, you find out who your friends really are. What's the point of hanging on to friends who do not support you by giving you the time, emotional or practical support that you need? If you're meeting up with a friend who constantly talks about themselves and their woes and doesn't even ask you about how you are and what's going on in your world (you know the selfish friends who don't care that you're going through a divorce because their problems are way bigger), why would you want to be friends with them?

Friendships take work and yes, you will find that you have to rekindle friendships that you have lost. You will find that friends drop by the wayside and go quiet after a divorce.

Once the novelty of asking you how you are and if you need anything wears off, they slowly disappear.

Not seeing friends that you saw in a couple with your ex is always tricky and can depend on who they were friends with before you met. Their loyalty will probably lie with that person regardless of who left who. People who are still in a marriage or long-term relationship don't often know what to say and it's just easier not to say anything. Losing friends is part of the territory of a divorce. You will feel as if you are walking around with a big sign on your head that says: "I am divorced, and I have no friends." So ....

Get new friends. Is this woman crazy? I hear you all saying, but just stop and think about it: new friends who do not know your history; new friends that you can start from scratch with; new friends who just accept who you are in this moment. I know you're shaking your head and saying, "How do I just get new friends? It's not as if I can pop into the supermarket and buy some." But I'm saying there are ways and means of getting a new crew. One of these is joining a social group in your local area. These are full of people who are probably going through a divorce and want to get out more instead of staring at four walls. You may decide to join a walking group or a book club or even a weekend restaurant group. There are so many different social groups out there if you know where to look. I met two new friends from a local social group. We got on famously and started to arrange nights out, coffee meet-ups, Sunday lunches and even a weekend away. It was great to have new friends as well as still having some of my old friends.

....

....

....

....

....

Your environment

Small steps

Change a few things around in your house. Move furniture, take down old pictures (it goes without saying that you take down the ones of you and your ex) and put up ones of you as this happy, confident and new single person. Get new throws, cushions or rugs to put your own stamp on what is now your own home.

Paint your bedroom. This seems odd, but you need to see your bedroom as your sanctuary, somewhere where you feel comfortable and safe – not lying awake at night remembering the arguments that you and your ex had, or the making up afterwards.

....

....

....

....

....

....

Big steps

Have a total house renovation. Knock down a few walls, add an extension, remodel the kitchen.

Move to a new house. This sounds like a huge step, but some people find that it helps them to move on as they are starting afresh in a new place that is without memories.

....

....

....

....

....

....

Your work/career

Small steps

Drive a different way to work.

Talk to people that you would not usually talk to.

Complete training or courses that are offered and that you find interesting.

Take something different for lunch. This is so simple but so empowering. Rock up to Costa and order a sundried tomato and mozzarella ciabatta instead of your usual ham and Emmental cheese toastie.

....

....

....

....

....

....

....

Big steps

Train in something new and start the path to a new career. I wouldn't have done any of this if it wasn't for my divorce. This proves that change can be the catalyst for growth and reinvention.

Go for that promotion that you have never thought about because you were married.

....

....

....

....

....

....

....

....

Your finances

Small steps

Try and save a little each month for your rainy-day fund or your new social life, because you are going to need it for all of the exciting things you are going to be doing!

See where you can save on your bills by swapping providers or getting a new phone contract.

Make a will and take out life insurance if you need to. I can't stress how important this is to give yourself peace of mind.

....

....

....

....

....

....

Big steps

See a financial adviser and overhaul your whole finances. This can be scary. You may realise that you are going to grow old and become a penniless pauper – but don't fear! The experts know what they are doing and can point you in the right direction and help you to make sound financial decisions.

Start saving for a once-in-a-lifetime trip or for a bigger deposit for a new house.

Open a cash ISA to add to your pension pot.

....

....

....

....

....

....

Your fun/spare time

Small steps

Try out a new hobby like pottery, art classes or sport.

Read a book – Yes, a whole one, you now have time!

Go to the cinema on your own – It's really easy to do as no one can see that you're a sad single person!

....

....

....

....

....

....

Big steps

Get on a random train and see where it takes you for a spontaneous day out. I used to do this all the time and went to some lovely places for the day.

Do something extreme like a bungee jump or a sky dive. Do it for charity and then you can't back out. I set myself the task of doing extreme things. I am thinking about walking over hot coals for my next challenge, or maybe not ....

....

....

....

....

....

....

I had a client who was struggling after their spouse had walked out and set up home with someone else.

They spent a lot of their day sleeping and couldn't get into any sort of routine. As we were all in lockdown at the time, they were working from home when required.

I didn't want to overwhelm them and make a daily plan, but we talked about just changing one small thing, whether that be cooking something healthy for breakfast or going out for a walk instead of their usual daily nap. We also talked about the benefits of building up to a daily timetable from setting the time they got up, ate, worked, walked, chill time to watch TV to the time they went to bed. That way they didn't have to think about it, they just had to do it!

Top Tip

Don't try and run before you can walk, start with something small and see where it takes you.

Do not beat yourself up if you wallow and don't make any changes, BUT, remind yourself that things will not change until you change them.

CHAPTER 11

Embrace

Single is no longer a lack of options – but a choice.
A choice to refuse to let your life be defined by your
relationship status but to live every day happily and let
your 'ever after' work itself out.

Mandy Hale

There is always a silver lining to every cloud. Yes, you're now single but being single brings such opportunities! I was 43 when my second marriage broke down (not exactly old but not fresh-faced and just out of college either).

The conversation that still sits in my mind was the one I had with my mum when I had asked her to babysit my daughter after my first marriage breakdown so that I could go on a night out. She said to me: "Fay, don't you think you ought to be staying at home to look after your daughter and not going out?"

This puzzled me as she loved babysitting and both my parents were a great support after both marriage breakdowns. I took a nanosecond to think about my answer, but replied: "Mum, I could spend my whole life dedicating every waking hour to my daughter and not having a social life and no friends, but when she is grown up and has flown the nest, where is that going to leave me?"

My mum couldn't answer that and it is something that I have carried with me. I wasn't going to be the sad, lonely spinster that had no life because I had dedicated it to bringing up my daughter.

I felt as if I still had a life to live and, boy, did I grab it – both times.

After moving into my new home with my children, after my second marriage breakdown, I couldn't believe the change that came over me. I decorated my new rooms, fixed the cistern (YouTube is great for that), bought myself a drill and put up my blinds. I felt invincible and said to myself, "Who needs a man? I can do this on my own." I bought things from the supermarket that my ex didn't like and cooked different meals. I watched exactly what I wanted to on TV and went to bed when I wanted to. I even started to sleep better as I had no one keeping me awake with their snoring.

Everything was now mine to take control of, no asking someone else, no having to compromise. When my children went to their dads', instead of sitting there twiddling my thumbs and stressing over what they were doing (I did feel a loss of control to begin with), I was out, making new friends; going to social groups; abseiling down cathedrals for charity; walking the Caminito del Rey, in Spain, and going down the fastest zip wire in England (although I nearly threw up afterwards). I even sat in the cinema on my own, because

I could and it felt liberating. I went out and stayed out all night (because I could). I would get trains and see where they went. I even booked myself on a yoga retreat abroad (yes, I know I keep going on about this but it was such a pivotal point in my break-up journey and I would encourage anyone and everyone to do it!) and loved every single minute of it. There was yoga in the morning, brunch with my fellow yogis and time in the afternoon to swim, sunbathe and wander around the local harbour before meeting again in the evening for meditation and a meal.

Did I miss my children? NO! I felt free. I started to feel as if my marriage had held me back. I felt that if I put my mind to it, I could do anything on my own. I didn't need a man to stand beside me. I think that if it wasn't for the love and care of my children, I can honestly say that I would have sold everything and gone off travelling and done the whole Julia Roberts thing in *Eat Pray Love,* which is in fact, a true story. I'm very jealous of the woman whose life that was based around. Even though I love my children dearly, I am already hatching my grand plan for when they have flown the nest and are adults. Although they are 16 and 10, so I've got a long wait. Impatient!

I'm not telling you that you should be reckless, but what I am saying is start to be selfish and put your needs at the top of the list (even if you have children. Well, only sometimes if you have children). Start to have fun and do things that you have always wanted to do but never did because you were in a relationship or married.

If this sounds scary, or batshit crazy to you, think about the alternative. Does it bear thinking about? Being in the same position, feeling the same negative emotions, feeling sorry for yourself and wondering what your ex is doing in twelve months or even two years' time? No, it doesn't!

Yes, of course it's going to be hard to carve out a life for yourself. It's even harder if you feel as if you don't deserve to be happy, but you have as much right as everyone else. So why not accept it?

Some days I used to feel as if the whole world was against me, that everything I did went wrong, and I used to say to myself: "OK, stop the bus now because I want to get off!"

Whenever I felt like this, I would say to myself: "I can do this. I am strong. I will overcome the challenges that I am facing." Usually I was driving my car.

You should now know, after reading this book, that it's OK to have bad days as long as the good days outweigh the 'get off the bus' days.

And on my good days I would be researching my next trip, my next challenge and planning out my social and dating life around when I was child-free. I began to love my single life and ended up loving myself in the process.

Top Tip

Write a bucket list or have a 'dream jar' of things that you have always wanted to do but couldn't because you were married. This could be visiting a new country, learning a new skill or even kissing a stranger on a night out!

CHAPTER 12

Dates

Bloody men are like bloody buses –
You wait for about a year
And as soon as one approaches your stop
Two or three others appear.
Wendy Cope

"What?" I hear you say. "Date again? Why in God's name would I want to do that?" Everyone who has ever been through a break-up always says that. I did.

I told my friends that if I ever lived with, or married, anyone again to slap me around the face! I've not done either yet. I was adamant that no man was ever going to mess up my life again. I know that I sound like a cold, heartless woman, but I'm quite nice when you get to know me, just ask my friends or boyfriend (although he'd probably agree with the statement).

I actually, couldn't wait to write this chapter. By the time I met the person who was right for me, I had dated solidly for eighteen months and what I didn't know about dating again as

=2t>

a forty-something woman, wasn't worth knowing. Catfishing, breezing, circular dating, ghosting, bread crumbing, slow fade and book marking became part of my everyday vocabulary. I lost count of the number of dates I had (that's another book entitled *101 Dates* and that is going to take some writing!). There were some absolutely shocking ones. I'll say no more.

A question I get asked a lot is: "How will I know when I am ready to date?"

Again, there is no 'one size fits all' answer, or hard and fast rule. When you feel you are ready, or just want to test the waters, dip your toe into the dating pool and if you don't like it, you can try again at a later date.

I've heard many stories (mostly bad) about people getting straight back on the horse after their long-term marriage or relationship has broken down. This is a risky business as it's just filling an emotional space that needs to be dealt with. I can remember going on a date with a guy for a drink and he spent the whole time talking about his ex, what she'd done and how crap he was feeling. I ended up giving him a very informal coaching session and when I asked him how long ago this had happened, he told me that they had only broken up the previous week. Yes, the previous week! To be honest, I knew straight away that he wasn't for me, but I wanted to get the most out of meeting someone new. I think he got far more from me than I did from him. He contacted me a few days later to say he wasn't over his ex (No! really?) and he didn't think he could carry on dating. In an odd way, I was happy that a date with me made him realise that he wasn't ready (I realise that this says a lot about me!) and this may happen to you also. Just be prepared to bolt (literally) if it all gets too much and don't be too harsh on yourself if you realise that you want time before you start to date again.

An exercise that I do with clients is called 'Design Your Ideal Partner'. Sounds great, doesn't it? I help people to think about what qualities – physical, emotional, social – they want in a partner and also what they do not want. This should be ingrained in your brain after your divorce and the lessons you have learned. Some of the things you do not want may be in the compromise column, but some will definitely be 'no goes'.

For instance, one of my biggest 'no goes' was smoking. I had made my mind up that I would not entertain dating a smoker, even if they looked like Tom Hardy. Both of my exes were smokers, one occasionally and the other one a 20-a-day kind of person, and I hated it!

Generally, people will find it quite easy to do the physical qualities but struggle a little with the emotional qualities, but this is where you have to use the lessons gained from your break-up. If your ex did not listen to you and understand you the way that you wanted, then putting 'empathetic' on your list would be a good idea.

Laughter may be high up on your list, so meeting someone who was funny and could make you laugh would be a bonus.

I always tell people that they are never going to get 100% of what they want in a partner. There is always going to be a compromise. As a good rule of thumb, getting 80% of what's on your ideal partner list is good!

Everyone has a 'want' list when they start dating. Sometimes it's very extensive, down to eye colour and what music they listen to. Alternatively, some people may just have 'needs to have a pulse'.

Now we need to be sensible and not get too hung up on our mental tick list. Use it as a guide only. The odds of finding someone who ticks every box is going to be slim. If by an amazing stroke of luck you do find them, you may be far more interested in them than they are in you.

Yes, before you ask, I had a mental tick list and would sit ticking off boxes during a date. But I always kept an open mind, even when a date I had turned up in his dirty and shabby work clothes. I figured that I needed to get to know the person behind the clothes, even though 'knows how to dress' was high on my list. Compromises always have to be made – a bit like buying a house. 'Nice house but small garden' kind of thing.

Sometimes you meet someone and the whole tick list gets thrown out of the window. They don't tick any boxes at all, but you can't help but like them, want to kiss them or even rip their clothes off! You can't quantify that elusive spark that everyone talks about and wants in their forever person.

When I met my partner, I was seriously thinking of taking a dating break. If you don't already know, dating is hard; it takes both time and energy. I had got a third date lined up with someone I had recently met, but I was taking my time to get to know him as I wasn't sure (he was good looking but our personalities didn't seem to match). I also felt that I didn't want to take up all my spare time with dating.

But as soon as I met my now partner, I knew that he was going to be a big part of my life and I couldn't explain why. I wasn't bothered about my tick list. If it works, it works. I didn't go on any more dates after that as I didn't want to muddy the waters. I wanted to put all my energies into seeing if this had legs and if it didn't work out then so be it. We are nearly at the two-year milestone now and planning our next travel adventure for when lockdown and travel restrictions have been lifted.

When I started internet dating, I have to admit that I wasn't really prepared for the amount of people on these apps. I realised that I was a very small fish in a very big pond of singletons. (Yes, I went on Plenty of Fish, or PoF for short, and boy was that an education!) If you're a woman, be prepared to get pictures of naked body parts, lewd comments and lots of messages from young men wanting an experienced, older women. These really made me laugh. Even though I was intrigued and slightly tempted, I wasn't into the whole 'Mrs Robinson' thing. I remember that some of the chat-up lines from these younger men made me want to tell their mothers; they are too explicit to put in this book.

If you're a man, be prepared for lots of pictures of women with filters on and doggy ears as well as Russian beauties trying to get you to sign up to their sites.

I also didn't really know what I wanted, who I wanted and how it was all going to pan out. I just knew that I wanted to meet new and interesting people and you will certainly do that if you go on dating apps. I certainly wasn't looking for husband number three.

So, why do people date after a separation or divorce?

- ♥ To feel attractive again.

- ♥ To meet new people.

- ♥ To have sex with someone else.

♥ To see what type of people they are attracted to.

♥ To find a partner to spend the rest of their life with.

You will know when the time is right. Go with your gut and don't listen to anyone else's advice.

I heard a story about a man who met his new partner at his wife's funeral. Allegedly, she worked for the undertaker and was part of the funeral procession. Urban myth? Who knows? But sometimes things happen when you least expect them to.

Many people make the mistake of throwing themselves into the first relationship that comes along. It's a way of stuffing all the hurt and emotional pain that you went through without having to deal with any of it. I'm sure you've all heard of rebound relationships.

People who do this convince themselves that they are happy (happy, they may be but are they really, 'core' happy?). Then, when it's all over in three, six or twelve months, they are left stunned wondering why they are in the same position again.

I am not saying don't do this. Rebounds are often a necessary part of recovery and moving forwards. I'm also not saying, become a member of a religious, celibate order. What I am saying is, be clear on the reason why you are dating. If it's just to feel attractive again, fine. If it's because you want to meet someone to have a one-night stand with, great. If it's because you're bored and want to fill the empty space, cool. If it's because you want to meet your soul mate, go for it! Just know your reasons and be honest about them when people ask you. It's OK to have a 'just right now' relationship.

I made the mistake of not being fully honest with someone I was dating nine months after my marriage breakdown.

I had moved to my new house by then and was taking full advantage of dating again. I met someone nice and thought, "Yeah, this is all right."

Over the weeks that passed, I met his family, went round at Christmas, you get the picture. What I didn't realise was that he was far more invested than I was. He had been single for a few years after his divorce and was at the stage where he was looking for his life partner. I realised that I was nowhere near ready for that. I didn't lie to him, but I wasn't overly forthcoming either (maybe because I wasn't sure myself). The turning point came when he met my parents, children and sister at a family meal. It totally freaked me out and I ended it a few days later. Reading between the lines he was hurt, and I got the feeling that he felt I had led him on. I felt a little guilty about that, but I had tried to be honest with him. The lesson here is, be aware that people will be on different pages and want different things. If you're newly single you may not want anything too committed. If you're a singleton expert you may want something more.

Dating in the twenty-first century is totally different from dating when I was a teenager. Meeting someone at the local youth club, or from across the road; waiting for hours for the said boy to turn up; waiting with another girl (much prettier than you) who is waiting for the same boy (of course that happened to me). Arranging to meet said boy the week after, asking your dad's permission to call said boy from the only telephone in the house and so on, and so on ....

Now, you can be swiping right, chatting and meeting someone all in the space of a day. And if you're totally on it, you can have two, three or four dates in twenty-four hours. It can be done. How do I know that?

Now some of you may be saying, "I'd rather meet someone on a night out, or in my everyday life, than have to resort to an app." That's your prerogative (I have a friend who prefers to do this and can't be bothered with dating apps). But, if you want that to happen you may be waiting a while. If you really want to meet that special person, internet dating gives you a huge pool to work from. My advice is, what have you got to lose?

I would never have met my partner in my day-to-day life in a million years. We live nearly an hour away from each other (that has its advantages), we have different jobs and move in totally different circles. He had never been to the town that I live in before he met me (I think he's regretting it now!) so the chances of us meeting were slim to zero But, we both swiped right on the same dating app.

I don't want to frighten you, but to get to this stage I dated like a boss. My friends couldn't keep up with me. I took full advantage of my singleton status. I learned so many valuable lessons from dating various people and met some great people who are still friends in the process. Did I make mistakes or trip up? Yes, of course I did but I don't regret anything that I did. Did I date guys who were not telling me the full story? Oh yes, but as I've said before you can't control the choices that other people make. They should have been more honest, but I didn't lose any sleep over it.

If the thought of internet dating terrifies you, drag a single friend along to a speed dating evening. These are great fun, and if you're not drunk by the end of it and crying into your drink because all the people there did not float your boat, you haven't lived!

I remember setting up my profile on a very popular dating app after getting back from a drunken night out with my girlie singleton friends and spending the rest of the night swiping and chatting. One guy suggested he come round for a drink as he didn't live too far away. No thank you – I'd put my pjs on!

So, if you're thinking about taking the plunge and signing up to an app, I have listed a few that I went on. Some you pay for and you may ask yourself why should I pay – especially if you don't find the right person for you? On the other hand, if you do, you'll think your investment was well worth it.

My advice is, pay for one app for a few months and choose two apps that are free. That way, you are giving yourself the best chance. So, in no particular order:

Match £ – This is a good starting app. Most of the people on here are genuine and looking for love. The only problem I found with this app was that I kept seeing the same selection of people. There didn't seem to be many newbies.

eharmony £ – This is for serious daters who want to find their forever person. The people on here are genuine. I didn't stay on here for long as I wasn't ready for my forever person.

EliteSingles ££ – This is an app for career-driven and independent singles. Apart from it being a tad expensive, a lot of the profile pictures were taken on the ski slopes, climbing a mountain or on their horse. I did connect with a few people, but they lived nowhere near me.

Zoosk £ – Zoosk is for people who don't like to follow the crowd. It's quirky, sporty and fun. The person I dated off here was not altogether transparent. I would go as far as to say he was a kitten fish (explained in the dating jargon later).

POF – Plenty of Fish is free and probably the most popular dating app. There are thousands of people on this app. It's great fun, as long as you don't expect too much. You will have the opportunity to speak to lots of people. Just be aware that some people on this app (and probably others) are not single in the true sense of the word.

Bumble – Bumble is a free app. It's for women who want to be in control of who contacts them. I admire the men on this app as they have to wait for the women to make the first move and if the woman does not make contact in twenty-four hours, the match disappears into the ether (a little bit like Russian roulette).

Tinder – This free app has had a serious image overhaul. It isn't just for people wanting a hook-up, but for people from all walks of life. Yes, there are a lot of young people on here, but my experience was a good one and I would advise anyone to go on it.

Dating Jargon

It really is a different language, but it will help you if you know the terms, especially if anyone asks you if you're into 'circular dating' or why you have 'ghosted' them.

These relatively new dating terms refer to what we used to call ignoring, lying, leading you on, abandonment, rejection, selfishness and cheating in both the physical and non-physical sense.

I'm not ashamed to say that I did some (not all of the things on this list) as well as being on the receiving end of most of them. It helps before you start dating to expect that some of these will probably happen to you. It's the nature of twenty-first century dating (rightly or wrongly). There are new terms coming out almost daily, so not all of them will be in here but here are a few that I know.

Catfishing

Catfishing is when someone pretends to be someone else online. They assume a different name, identity and will even post fake pictures on their profile. They know exactly what to do and what to say to hook their victim and reel them in. They will go the extra mile and message, text and email you frequently and make you believe that they are interested. The best way to expose a catfish is to ask them to Skype you or Snapchat you. They will come up with 101 reasons why they can't and make it sound believable. Many catfishers will go on to ask you to lend them some money. If you get to this stage with a catfisher, block them!

Kitten Fishing

This term is relatively new and means lying. It is when someone presents themselves on an app in an unrealistic way, whether that is lying about their age, what they do (to look more of a catch) or posting highly-edited or old photos of themselves that are not a true likeness.

Bread Crumbing

This term is used for when people keep you dangling on a string. They send you out tiny bits of flirtation and rewards (whether that is a picture or a message to keep you interested in them) for when they want to engage. You will hear from them every few days but no more. It makes me wonder why people do this. For an ego boost or 'just because'? I once messaged a guy who I knew had been doing this to ask him if he had nothing better to do.

Slow Fade

A slow fade is what it says on the tin: you get lots of messages, calls and dates and then slowly but surely nothing. This can be worse than ghosting as it gives you hope that whatever it was can recover or develop again. A slow fade happens because the person doing the fading does not want the discomfort of having a difficult conversation with the person they have been interacting with. Slow fading happens a lot on dating apps and even after months of dating. It comes with the territory unfortunately and you just have to suck it up and carry on. If someone does this to you, you may feel that you want closure or an explanation but in reality, you're probably not going to get one.

Circular Dating

I personally love this term and did a lot of it (I'm owning up to this one). It means that you are dating about three people at once with the intention of finding the one. When I say 'dating', I do not mean sleeping with or being committed, as this would be far too complicated. I am talking about coffee and dinner dates, meeting up for a stroll or going to the pub. I'm talking about dating people in a casual way to see how you get on and finding out whether it could develop. I did this a lot and I was always honest with my dates that I was having dates with other people. When I did find the one, I stopped dating other people immediately as I wanted to see how it would develop and it has. You will know when you get to this stage.

Ghosting and Zombieing

Ghosting is when you are messaging someone, talking to someone, dating someone or even in a micro-relationship with someone, and all of a sudden they cut all contact without any explanation. Even if you try and contact them, they will not respond and will block you from trying. If you are ghosted, there is usually a reason why and to be honest it can stem from the other person not wanting to justify or explain why they don't want to carry on. You are left feeling confused and hurt (especially if you thought it was going somewhere). You may feel as if you need some sort of closure or explanation, but the truth is, you're probably not going to get one. My tip is, keep telling yourself that you are better off without them. You deserve better than being ghosted by someone that you liked.

Zombieing is when the ghost appears again (yes, from the dead). This could be weeks or months after they have ghosted you and act as if nothing has happened. Yes, there may have been a valid reason for them to ghost you but a quick text at the time would have been a far better way to explain themselves.

I am not telling you what to do in this situation as I think you know. And by then you will have forgotten their name!

Bookmarking

When someone has bookmarked you, they are keeping you on the bench in case their preferred choice isn't available. Or, if they agree to a date, but don't seem to be able to commit to when, they are hanging on to see if they can get a date with someone else first before committing to a date with you. This will happen a lot at the weekend. Sometimes, your date can only commit to a daytime date instead of an evening date. Is there anything wrong with this? If you're 'breezing', it won't bother you as when you have wowed them over a lunchtime coffee, they will be putting you in their prime time Saturday night slot! If you're circular dating, your favourite date will fill your top date slot and the others will fit around it. So, in essence you are bookmarking the other two.

Serial Dater

A serial dater is a person who just loves dating and doesn't play by the rules. After dating one person (a few times) they move on to the next. Serial daters love the 'high' that dating new people gives them. They don't want to be tied down and will move through dates and micro-relationships very quickly.

I have to be honest and say that many people who I dated asked me if I was a serial dater. I honestly think the term 'serial dater' gets bandied about a lot. I was dating for a while and I had dates with lots of people and a few micro-relationships, so if that makes me a serial dater then I hold my hands up to it! But I didn't date with the intention of being a serial dater. I didn't want to settle for someone who was OK for me. I wanted someone who was right for me.

I dated a lot because I didn't meet the right person for me. I wasn't going to commit to the first person that showed an interest. I was dating as a way of finding out what I wanted in a person. You're very lucky to meet your forever person on your first date. I didn't, and I had to date different people to find him.

The one thing that I would advise, if you are starting to date, is know what you want and the type of relationship that is going to make you happy. Knowing what you want is not being needy or high maintenance; it is setting your boundaries and allowing yourself to have the relationship that you want and deserve.

Breezing

I advise anyone who is dating after a divorce or long-term partnership to do this. When you are breezing, you are not over-thinking what is happening; you are taking each day as it comes, having fun and not obsessing about what the other person is doing. You have the attitude 'If it happens it happens'. It's all about dating someone (or a few people) and being chilled about it all. Don't worry why they haven't texted you, or if they're on a date with someone else. That's their prerogative until you have the chat about being exclusive.

When you're breezing, you are not getting too emotionally invested in the person straight away. So, if, and when, it ends you can say: "Yes, it was fun but I'm now moving on."

My dos and don'ts of internet dating

Don't blame me if you don't take heed of my advice. It's a dog-eat-dog world on dating apps, but if you're prepared you won't trip up or – even worse – get hurt. We've already got that T-shirt!

Dos

Do post a variety of pictures that allow someone to see who you truly are. I had one date that said that if people did not have a full body picture on their profile, he wouldn't meet them as they were obviously large (yes this is very rude, and I didn't see him again). I'm not saying put a full-length picture on but just a variety of shots other than your passport photo!

Do write a short paragraph to go with your pictures. Draft it out (you can always add it later after your friends have given it the once-over). Include a few things that you want from a date and a few things about yourself. For example:

Quirky, sassy, fun, single mum of two children looking for someone to laugh and go on long walks with. Not looking for a one-night stand (ONS, in case you come across this abbreviation). *But happy to date and see where it goes, Not interested in smokers.*

My profile was slightly similar. Keep it short. If you write an extensive list of what you want, people may think you're too picky. You may be, (you should be!) but you don't want to scare people off!

Do talk to as many people as you want. There is no rule and you will quickly find out who you are more connected to.

Do swap numbers when you feel the time is right. You will find out very quickly if you get on during a phone call. I made the mistake of texting someone for weeks and when we eventually called each other I did not like his accent and the connection that I thought was there, wasn't. After that, I would always call someone before a date. Just to see if they could string two sentences together.

Don'ts

Don't post a picture of your children on your profile. They didn't ask to be on there and it's not something that you would want your ex to find out about.

Don't post a picture of your dog instead of yourself. So many people do this, and you have to ask yourself why? Do they have a large nose or are they still married?

Don't use old pictures on your profile. Yes you look good, but your date is going to get a shock when you eventually meet, and you look ten years older.

Don't lie about your age! So many people do this and you're only setting yourself up for a fall if you hit it off and then drop it into the conversation months down the line.

Don't post pictures without a write-up. It doesn't have to be *War and Peace*. I had a rule that if there was no write-up, I wasn't interested as they came across as not being bothered.

Don't assume that the person you're talking to is only talking to you. Accept that they are talking to six other people at the same time (as you will be or should be). I had one guy who called me out over talking to other people. I was honest when he asked me if I was talking to anyone else and he got all shirty when I told him that I was, as he was only talking to me. We didn't get to a telephone conversation!

Top Tip

Be truthful about what stage you are at and what you are after. Your dates will respect you more for it.

Chill out, have fun and enjoy the process. It's OK to have a 'just right now' person while you're waiting for your 'forever' person.

CHAPTER 13

Re-start

You can't start the next chapter of your life if you keep re-reading the last one.

Michael McMillian

I feel quite emotional writing this chapter, because when you eventually get to this stage you will have been put through the wringer in more ways than one. You may have started a few new books, only to close them again and start another one, but hopefully you will have had some fun, learned more about yourself than ever before and be well on the way to happiness, acceptance and fulfilment.

You will be a totally different, and hopefully better, person. You will be able to look at yourself in the mirror and say, "Yeah, you're OK and not doing a bad job of life; I actually like you."

When I think about the dark place I was in a few years ago, it makes me shudder that I was even in that situation. I don't ever want to be in that place again. I don't like to dwell on it for too long.

I was coaching a client who had started to date again, and on the face of it, was happy. But they realised that they were not over their ex and their new relationship fell apart. They had used this new relationship to mask what they were truly feeling and used it as a coping mechanism. They felt like they had failed and would never be happy again. They wanted to get to a place of happiness without dealing with the aftermath first. They didn't think that they were strong enough to reach the top of their mountain. Unfortunately, recovery doesn't work like that; we can't just flick a switch and have everything be OK. Climbing the recovery mountain is one of the hardest things you may ever do.

I honestly think that I am who I am today because of my experiences and for that I am thankful. I wouldn't have come this far with a small nudge. I needed to go through the fire like a phoenix!

When will you be ready to close the book? I can't answer that. But I think that by now you have learned that you can't truly start a new one until you have. If I'm really being honest, do you ever really close the book? Yes, you do, but you may find that you take a peek back into the old one every now and again. If you can do that without it affecting you in a negative way, and be able to reflect on the lessons you have learned, then you know that you are ready.

Funnily enough, during lockdown I have been doing a bit of tidying (as everyone has) and I came across a large box of old photos of my second wedding (why do we women get lumped with the old wedding pics?), holidays, photos of my children as youngsters – all photos that I had not seen in a long time. I was able to look through them and reflect on the past without getting triggered or feeling worthless. I felt happy that I am now where I want to be in life (well, world domination is next on the cards) and I feel blessed. I couldn't ask for anything more. Your journey, like mine, will be hard, difficult, fraught with pitfalls and mistakes but with great learning opportunities and the potential for huge growth.

Top Tip

Don't rush to close the book until you are ready, and you will know when you are.

So, what now?

You have got all the tools you need to climb your own mountain and be successful in life and love. You just need to start your own book and make it the best book you have ever read! And don't worry if you have to rip a page or two out, start again and make it better!

"What we find in a soulmate is not something wild to tame but something wild to run with."

Robert Brault

ACKNOWLEDGEMENTS

There have been so many people who have been pivotal in helping me along my journey from supporting me through both my break-ups; giving me encouragement and advice when starting my business; pushing myself to be the best person I can be through to writing this book.

These people have touched my life in so many ways and for that I feel truly blessed.

The list is partly in a chronological order, and some are no longer with us. There are too many people to list from all the wonderful people I call my friends to people that I have met only briefly. Thank you, everyone.

My mum and dad, who have been married for over fifty years and stood by each other in sickness and in health.

Mavis Rice and Jackie Chapman, who were my rocks throughout my divorces.

My sister- and brother-in-law, Emma and Shane Scott, who helped me move house both times and were always at the end of the phone.

Sara Thomas and Emma Parker, who were always there when I thought I was falling apart, even though they had their own mountains to climb.

Liz Hook, for allowing me to use her story and for being one of my first clients. I am proud of how far you have come!

Sarah Davison, Divorce Coach – my mentor and tutor. If it wasn't for you, I would never have started my own business.

Jo Hopton and Barbara Parker – my wonderful and crazy break-up buddies, who were with me on my dating journey – the fun we had!

Sarah at Goldcrest Books, who shared my vision and helped me to make the right choices to make my book the best that it could be!

Elaine at Caittom Publishing, who turned my ramblings into something wonderful!

Natalie at NB Photography, for my author's picture.

Lucy and Toby – my wonderful children, who have spurred me on to be the best mum that I can be as well as a better person. I am so proud of how you have grown, and are still growing, and how you have coped and adapted to all the change that has been thrown at you. But most of all I am proud of how you have continued to support, love and annoy each other. **#thethreemusketeers #anythingispossibleifyouputyourmindtoit.**

Paul who never doubted my abilities, who has encouraged and supported me to achieve and follow my own path, who has walked beside me all the way and who has taught me that even after everything, you can find true happiness.

ABOUT THE AUTHOR

Fay is a single mum of two children from Burton upon Trent. She has been a primary school teacher for over twenty years and is also a relationship, infidelity and divorce coach.

She set up her own coaching company called *Feel Positive – Relationship, Infidelity and Divorce Coaching*, after going through two divorces and overcoming trauma, infidelity and abuse. Fay turned her life around, changing from someone who did not know how to function as a normal human being, after suffering low self-worth, anxiety, panic attacks and CPTSD, to being the most confident, driven, happy and fulfilled person she has even been.

She partly credits this to yoga, mindfulness, daily gratitude and learning to love herself again.

She is passionate about helping people in all areas of their relationships, whether that is rebuilding trust after infidelity to moving forwards and healing after a relationship breakdown. Fay coaches clients and couples all over the UK and also offers 'walk and talk' therapy around the National Forest, close to where she lives.

When she is not teaching or coaching, Fay loves yoga, walking, travel, pushing herself to experience new things and learn something new each day.

To contact the author, book a session or follow her on social media:

www.feelpositivecoaching.com

feelpositivecoaching@gmail.com

Instagram: feelpositivecoaching

Facebook: Feel Positive Coaching

Twitter: @FayPetcher

07821 109751